Dear Son

The god within you

William McLeod

A FATHER'S WISDOM
FOR LIFE'S JOURNEY

© 2025 Bill McLeod

ISBN: 978-1-77835-501-1 Paperback

All rights reserved, including the right to reproduce this book or portions thereof in any form whatsoever. Apart from any fair dealing for the purpose of research, private study, criticism or review, no part of this publication may be reproduced, stored in or introduced into a retrieval system, or transmitted in any form or by any means (electronic, mechanical, photocopying, recording or otherwise), without the prior written permission of the copyright owner.

To my mother, Rosemary,

Though we had only a brief time together, you have always been a part of me. Your love and spirit live within me, guiding my steps and shaping the person I've become. This book is not only a reflection of the lessons I've learned and the legacy I wish to leave but also a tribute to the strength and love you gave me, even in our short time together.

You are forever with me, in every word, every thought, and every moment.

With love,
Your son, Billy

Contents

Preface: Why I Wrote This Book vii
Chapter 1: The Shift Begins 1
Chapter 2: The Shift 5
Chapter 3: The Clues 11
Chapter 4: Laws of the Universe 17
Chapter 5: Emotions That Raise and Lower Frequency . . . 49
Chapter 6: The Power of Action 75
Chapter 7: Chapter: Self-Worth, Success, and Frequency . . 81
Chapter 8: Reflection and Legacy 87
Chapter 9: Odd Thoughts. 91
Chapter 10: Do You Believe in Magic? 99
Conclusion: Final Thoughts and Words. 107
Acknowledgments. 111
About the Author 113

Preface

Why I Wrote This Book

THERE COMES A point in life where we stop and look back at the wins, the losses, the lessons, and yes, even the missteps. We realize that much of what we've learned didn't come from a textbook, a degree, or the advice society throws at us. No, the real lessons came from life itself, from living through the highs and lows, and from those quiet moments where it all started to make sense (or didn't, but you kept going anyway).

This book is a reflection of that journey. It's not just about what I've learned; it's a love letter to you, my sons. You've watched me evolve, sometimes gracefully, sometimes clumsily, but always trying. I want to pass on the lessons I wish I had understood sooner; so that as you continue your own paths, you have a few extra tools in your toolbox.

When I began this journey, I had a head full of ideas and beliefs that I held tightly onto, still do in fact. But here's the thing: it wasn't always easy to share these ideas with you, especially when you were young. We were going through some tough transitions as a family, and I was dealing with my own battles, both with stress and health. To be honest, I wasn't sure if you'd ever fully understood how my mind worked or why I made some of the choices I made. It's not like we could sit down and have a three-hour conversation about my inner world, it was just too much. I didn't know if you were ready to hear it, or if I was even ready to explain it.

That's when Dear Son started to take shape. I figured if I couldn't talk it out, maybe I could write it down. In 2015, while living on Cedar Street in Woodstock, Ontario, I started scribbling notes, thinking, "One day, this will make sense." I wanted to write down everything I had been thinking, the lessons that helped me; and the ideas that shifted my life. If nothing else, I wanted to give you something you could read at your own pace, something that might explain why I made certain choices, even if we never had that deep talk over a Mio or sugar free Red Bull.

The truth is; I didn't always think this way. Like most people, I went through periods of frustration and self-doubt. There were times when life felt like it was happening to me instead of for me. You know what I mean, those days when it feels like the universe has it out for you. But everything changed when I realized that I was shaping my own reality with my thoughts, emotions, and actions. That realization didn't come easy, and I'm still working on it every day.

I've been influenced by so many teachers, books, and ideas that completely changed how I see the world. From the Law of Attraction to the power of gratitude, I've learned that life isn't just something you survive, it's something you create.

As I look back, I want to share those lessons with you. This book isn't meant to be a "how-to" guide on life (trust me, I'm still figuring it out myself). It's more like a collection of stories, lessons, and ideas that have transformed my journey, and maybe, just maybe, they'll help you along yours.

One thing I want to be clear about: this book isn't about perfection. It's about progress. It's about making choices and understanding that the energy you bring into every decision shapes what you get out of it. I'm still learning, still growing, and still applying these lessons in my life, so don't expect a flawless roadmap. We're in this together, figuring it out as we go.

Thank you for picking this up. Whether you're my sons or someone else reading this, my hope is that you find something in these pages that speaks to you. Maybe it'll shift your mindset, maybe it'll spark a new idea, or maybe it'll give you the nudge you need to take action on that thing you've been putting off. We're all on this journey together, and I'm incredibly grateful to be sharing mine with you.

With gratitude,
Dad

Chapter 1

The Shift Begins

DEAR SONS,

There's one belief that's shaped my journey more than anything else: the understanding that we are all connected to something greater, a higher power. Call it God, the Universe, or whatever feels right to you. For me, it's that quiet voice that reminds us we're not alone and that there's a force out there guiding us. But here's the kicker: we are also creators. Yep, that's right, you and me. We shape our lives through our thoughts, actions, and the energy we bring into the world.

This book isn't just a collection of lessons or motivational quotes I've gathered over the years (though, trust me, I've got plenty of those). This is my journey, messy, chaotic, beautiful, and most importantly, real. It's the story of the struggles, breakthroughs, and the moments that made me stop and say, "Wow, I get it now."

Watching you guys grow into the incredible young men you are has been one of my life's greatest joys. But I'd be lying if I said I've had all the answers along the way. Like you, I've stumbled, more than once. I've experienced times of doubt, frustration, and failure. But through it all, I discovered something powerful: we're never just along for the ride. We are active participants in shaping our lives. That's the lesson I hope you take from this chapter.

The Journey Before the Shift

Let me take you back for a second. My childhood wasn't exactly a fairytale. I lost my mother when I was a baby, and from then on, life felt like a series of losses. My father, God bless him, had his own demons, alcoholism and the kind of temper that didn't exactly lend itself to warm father-son moments. As you can imagine, this shaped the way I viewed the world for a long time.

I grew up in an environment where emotions were a sign of weakness. So, I built walls. I didn't cry. I didn't complain. I definitely didn't ask for help. If life was hard, I figured that's just the way it was. You sucked it up, pushed forward, and waited for the next storm to hit. In fact, I was so conditioned to expect bad luck that I would almost anticipate it, like waiting for the other shoe to drop.

I wasn't thriving. I was surviving. Life was about getting through it, not about creating something better. Relationships? Strained. Finances? Tight. Self-worth? Let's just say it wasn't where it needed to be.

I even reached a point where I wondered if you boys might be better off without me. It was a dark time, but looking back now, I see it as the moment before the shift. Sometimes, you have to hit the lowest point to find the strength to climb out.

The Turning Point: Discovering the Law of Attraction

In 2017, things began to change. That was when I was introduced to The Secret, a book that turned my world upside down. The idea behind the Law of Attraction seemed almost too simple: like attracts like. Your thoughts, feelings, and beliefs shape the reality you experience. At first, I'll admit, I thought, "Really? It's that easy?" But when you've spent most of your life feeling like the universe is out to get you, this idea was a lifeline.

I wasn't skeptical, though, I was ready. I needed a change, and this idea gave me the hope I was looking for. The more I dove into the concept, the more I realized just how often I had been focusing on lack, fear, and negativity. Guess what that got me? More lack, fear, and negativity.

But what if I shifted my focus? What if I deliberately put my energy into what I wanted, instead of what I feared? It was a radical shift, but it was exactly what I needed.

Embracing the Shift

Slowly but surely, I started practicing the Law of Attraction. I paid attention to the words I used. I stopped saying things like "I'll never catch a break" and replaced them with affirmations like "Good things are on their way."

It wasn't just about wishful thinking. I began aligning my thoughts, words, and actions with the life I wanted to create. And guess what? The universe responded. Little by little, I started seeing positive changes. Opportunities I hadn't noticed before began to reveal themselves. Life wasn't perfect, but it was shifting.

One of the biggest changes happened within me. I stopped waiting for the other shoe to drop and started believing in possibility again. That old version of me, the one who expected the worst, began to fade away. In its place was someone who believed I had the power to create my own reality, and that the universe wasn't out to get me. In fact, it was working with me.

Why I'm Writing This for You

Now, sons, here's the reason I'm writing all this down. I want you to understand that you are never a victim of your circumstances. No matter what life throws at you, you always have the power to shape your reality. You're not stuck in a role that life hands you. You're the writer, director, and star of your own story.

I didn't fully understand these principles when I was your age, and I don't want you to wait as long as I did to figure them out. This book is about the lessons I've learned along the way, the ones that helped me shift from survival mode to a life full of purpose and meaning. I hope that by sharing these lessons, you'll be able to navigate your own journey with a little more clarity and confidence.

Here's the truth: Life will throw curveballs your way. But you have the power to decide how you respond. You can either focus on the obstacles or look for the opportunities hidden within them. The choice is yours. And believe me, it's a powerful choice.

With love and gratitude,
Dad

Chapter 2

The Shift

BEFORE I DISCOVERED the Law of Attraction, I wasn't where or who I wanted to be. Life seemed to throw obstacle after obstacle my way, and no matter how hard I tried, I often felt trapped. I thought the problem was everything around me, life, circumstances, other people, but it took me years to realize the real issue was my own mindset and, in many ways, my unresolved anger.

Early Years: The Trap of Anger and Control

Growing up, I didn't learn healthy ways to deal with emotions. My father, bless him, had his struggles, and he controlled situations through anger and fear. As a kid, I internalized that approach, thinking, "This is how you gain respect. This is how you make people listen."

Anger became my default mode, my tool for controlling situations, especially in my 20s, 30s, and even into my 40s. I thought that anger was strength, that if I let people see my rage, they'd respect me. In social situations, especially if I felt disrespected, my temper would flare up fast, and I saw fighting as a way to defend my honor. Looking back, I can see how unpredictable I must have seemed to my friends. I'd show up to a nice gathering and, without warning, be ready to fight.

For a long time, I didn't even think I had a problem. If I felt disrespected, anger seemed like the most reasonable response. I believed that reacting with rage made me more of a man, more in control. But I realize now that it wasn't control, it was chaos. There were moments when my temper got so bad, I'd almost blackout from the intensity of my rage. In those moments, I wasn't in control at all; I was a slave to my emotions. I couldn't see it then, but I see it now.

In hindsight, I can understand why people started distancing themselves from me. Though good people, my friends began leaving me out of certain situations, and it wasn't hard to figure out why. They saw me as unpredictable. I'd walk into a room, and they never knew if we'd be having a great time or if I'd pick a fight with someone over the slightest disrespect. I wouldn't have wanted to be around me either.

Observing Rather Than Reacting

As time went on, and after being introduced to the Law of Attraction, I realized something profound. Instead of trying to be involved in every situation or taking everything personally, I found myself stepping back. I started observing people more, paying attention to their emotions and the energy they brought into a room. This wasn't something I had done before. I was usually so consumed by my own reactions and feelings that I didn't take the time to notice the vibrations others were sending out.

This shift, from reacting to observing, was crucial for me. I stopped interpreting everything as a personal attack and started seeing things for what they were. Sometimes, people were just dealing with their own stuff, and it had nothing to do with me. This new approach allowed me to maintain my calm and avoid unnecessary conflict.

We'll touch more on this later when we talk about frequency, but understanding the vibrations and emotions people carry is a powerful tool. It helped me realize that not everything required my emotional investment or reaction. In fact, most situations benefited more from quiet observation than heated involvement.

Logic Before Emotion

Another major part of my shift was learning to put logic before emotion. This was a lesson I carried not only into my personal life but also into my work, especially when I started teaching policing students. I would always emphasize the importance of approaching situations with clear, logical thinking before letting emotions take over. It wasn't about suppressing emotions, it was about understanding them and making sure they didn't cloud judgment.

When I started combining logic with the principles of the universe, the laws of frequency, energy, and vibration, my whole perspective on life changed. Suddenly, I could see patterns in how people talked and acted, and I could almost predict where they were in their lives based on the energy they put out. The way someone speaks often reveals the state of their mind and what they're attracting into their life, whether they know it or not.

The Shift in Perspective: An Eye-Opening Conversation

I'll never forget an eye-opening moment after a hockey game one day. I was playing with a group of lawyers and doctors, and during our post-game chat, I mentioned I wanted to leave policing to aim for something bigger, something with no ceiling. I expected skepticism, but these men, well-established and financially secure, were supportive. They told me it was a great idea and encouraged me to pursue it.

It reminded me of a principle I later read in Steven Siebold's *177 Mental Toughness Secrets of the World Class*. Siebold explains that world-class thinkers operate with a mindset of abundance, always looking for possibilities and solutions, while the masses focus on fear and scarcity. This conversation illustrated that perfectly. The same discussion I had with people living paycheck to paycheck was met with a completely different response. Instead of encouragement, I was told I was crazy and irresponsible for thinking that way. It wasn't just about their financial situation, it was about their mindset. They couldn't see beyond their current limitations, and in their eyes, aiming for something higher seemed reckless.

This experience drove home how much our beliefs shape our reality. When you align with a mindset of abundance, you see opportunities where others see risks.

Letting Go of Anger

Anger had been my constant companion for so long, I didn't know who I'd be without it. Discovering the Law of Attraction was the turning point. I began to see how much my thoughts and emotions shaped my reality. The principle of 'like attracts like' made me confront a hard truth: my years of focusing on negativity, along with my anger, had only drawn more of the same into my life.

I wasn't just stuck because of external events, I was stuck because I kept choosing anger. Every time I let it take over, I fueled a cycle of fear, disrespect, and isolation. I wasn't in control; my emotions were. Until I could take charge of my own mind, peace, respect, and the life I wanted were out of reach."

The Shift: Embracing the Law of Attraction

In 2017, I came across The Secret, and it was a revelation. I realized that if I wanted to change my life, I had to change my thoughts, my emotions, and the energy I was putting out into the world. I was tired of feeling trapped in the same cycle, and the Law of Attraction felt like the escape hatch I needed.

I started practicing this new mindset. It wasn't easy, and old habits didn't die quickly. But little by little, I stopped responding to challenges with anger and started asking myself, "What if I don't let this get to me? What if I handle this differently?" Those were radical thoughts for me. After years of thinking anger was power, I had to learn that real strength came from controlling my emotions, not letting them control me.

Replacing Anger with Gratitude and Positivity

Once I began to see anger for what it was, a destructive force that was driving people away and holding me back, I knew I needed to replace it with something better. That's where gratitude came in. Every time I felt that old wave of anger rising, I'd stop and try to focus on something for which I was grateful no matter how small. It was like rewiring my brain, little by little.

I started catching myself before reacting. Instead of letting negative thoughts build into rage, I'd challenge them. I'd ask, "What's the lesson here? How can I respond in a way that brings something positive?" That wasn't easy at first, but with time, it became my new way of thinking.

I realized that problems weren't just obstacles; they were challenges from which I could learn. Instead of using anger as a weapon, I began using calmness and clarity as tools for handling difficult situations. The more I did this, the more control I felt over my own life.

Chapter 3

The Clues

NOW THAT I had decided to pursue the Law of Attraction and the idea of the universe working in harmony with our desires, I needed proof. Sure, I'd read books and; watched videos, and all the ideas sounded great. But my mind was still in detective mode, demanding more. After all, I spent years as a police officer, a career built on facts, evidence, and proof. Naturally, my inner detective kicked in: Show me the clues!

It wasn't enough for me to hear about it from gurus or motivational speakers. I wanted to see if there was historical backing, real-world examples, and personal stories that tied into the Law of Attraction. I wasn't content with surface-level inspiration. I needed to dig deeper. If the Law of Attraction was as powerful as people said, there had to be clues scattered throughout history, scripture, and the lives of people who had experienced its effects.

That's when I started looking, really looking, and what I found surprised me. The clues were there, scattered across time and culture, hidden in plain sight like Easter eggs in a blockbuster movie. The concept of manifesting your desires, attracting what you think about, and aligning with a higher energy has been with us for centuries. The more I dug, the more I realized that people have been tapping into this power for as long as we've been walking upright.

Clues from the Bible

One of the first places I turned to for clues was the Bible. Whether you're religious or not, the Bible has some strong lessons that resonate with the Law of Attraction. And I couldn't ignore the fact that many verses mirrored the same ideas I was learning about the universe and energy. It's like finding the Law of Attraction's "greatest hits" in one of the world's oldest texts.

Read Matthew 7:7-8 (NIV): "Ask, and it will be given to you; seek, and you will find; knock, and the door will be opened to you. For everyone who asks receives; the one who seeks finds; and to the one who knocks, the door will be opened." That's the Law of Attraction in action. If you actively seek something, whether it's a new opportunity, a change in life, or a fresh start, you'll find it. The universe responds to what you're focused on. It's basically saying, "Ask, and the universe will reply, 'Sure, let's make that happen.'"

Another verse that hit home was Mark 11:24 (NIV): "Therefore I tell you, whatever you ask for in prayer, believe that you have received it, and it will be yours." I love this one because it emphasizes belief. It's not enough to ask, you have to believe it's already yours. That's faith. That's exactly how the Law of Attraction operates. It's like placing an order with the universe but knowing deep down that the delivery truck is already on the way.

Then there's Luke 6:38 (NIV): "Give, and it will be given to you. A good measure, pressed down, shaken together and running over, will be poured into your lap. For with the measure you use, it will be measured to you." Translation: What you give out is what you get back. You radiate positivity, love, gratitude, and guess what comes back? A whole lot of the same. It's basically the universe saying, "I got your back, as long as you've got mine."

Matthew 13:12 (NIV) takes it further: "Whoever has will be given more, and they will have an abundance. Whoever does not have, even what they have will be taken from them." That's a profound reminder that what you focus on grows. Focus on abundance, and more will flow your way. Focus on lack, and that scarcity mindset will pull more away. The universe doesn't care whether it's positive or negative, whatever you focus on, it magnifies. So, choose wisely.

Historical Figures Who Knew "The Secret"

After diving into religious texts, I wanted to see if there were any historical heavyweights who understood this concept. I wasn't disappointed. As it turns out, some of the greatest minds in history had been dropping clues about the Law of Attraction long before anyone had labeled it.

Take Nikola Tesla, for example. The man was a genius, not only in science but in understanding energy. He once said, "If you want to find the secrets of the universe, think in terms of energy, frequency, and vibration." That's the Law of Attraction in a nutshell. Tesla knew that everything in the universe, including our thoughts, operates on frequencies and vibrations. He wasn't just talking about electricity, he was talking about life itself. You want to attract something? Tune in to its frequency.

Then there's Albert Einstein. He famously said, "Imagination is everything. It is the preview of life's coming attractions." Einstein knew the power of imagination. What you think about, what you visualize, is a sneak peek of what's to come. The universe responds to your imagination. It's almost as if Einstein was saying, "Whatever you're dreaming about, the universe is already building it for you."

Let's not forget Buddha, who taught, "What you think, you become." His teachings reflect the very essence of the Law of Attraction, your thoughts shape your reality. It's not just positive thinking; it's a profound understanding of how our mental state creates our external world.

Modern Celebrities Who Practice the Law of Attraction

Now, let's jump forward to modern times, where plenty of well-known celebrities are practicing the Law of Attraction, often without calling it that. It's not just self-help gurus who talk about manifesting desires, many people you know and admire attribute their success to these principles.

Jim Carrey is one of my favorite examples. Before he became a superstar, he wrote himself a $10 million check for "acting services rendered," dated it for Thanksgiving 1995, and carried it around in his wallet. He visualized his success long before it happened. In 1994, he got the lead role in Dumb and Dumber, and guess how much he was paid? Yep, $10 million. That's not a coincidence, that's the Law of Attraction in action.

Oprah Winfrey, arguably one of the most successful people on the planet, openly credits the Law of Attraction for her success. Oprah talks about focusing on gratitude and abundance, and how the universe responds by bringing more of those things into her life. She's living proof that what you put out into the world comes back to you in spades.

Will Smith, another powerhouse, talks about belief and visualization. He says, "In my mind, I've always been an A-list Hollywood superstar. Y'all just didn't know it yet." He believed in his success long before anyone else did. That's the Law of Attraction at work, he visualized, he believed, and the universe delivered.

And then there's Denzel Washington. Denzel often talks about faith, gratitude, and speaking your dreams into existence. He once said, "Put God first. In everything you do, if you believe, and put in the work, you will achieve success." That's the Law of Attraction, right there. His success, grounded in faith and belief, is proof that when you align with a higher energy and work toward your goals, the universe moves mountains to make it happen.

Steve Harvey is another great example. He has openly talked about his struggles before making it big and how he used faith and visualization to transform his life. He says, "If you can see it in your mind, you can hold it in your hand." Steve didn't just dream about success, he saw it, believed in it, and worked tirelessly until it became his reality. His story is proof that no matter where you start, if you align your energy and thoughts with what you desire, the universe will make a way.

Conclusion: The Secret Has Always Been There

As I looked for clues, I realized that the Law of Attraction isn't some new-age concept or modern-day fad. It's been around for centuries, embedded in religious texts, practiced by the greatest minds in history, and understood by modern-day success stories. The signs are everywhere if you're willing to look.

For me, this was the confirmation I needed. The Law of Attraction is real, and it's been quietly guiding us all along. The universe responds to our thoughts, beliefs, and energy, and history has been leaving us clues about this for generations. The question is: Are we willing to recognize them and use that knowledge to shape our lives?

Chapter 4

Laws of the Universe

WHEN I FIRST learned about the Laws of the Universe, it was like discovering the final piece of a puzzle I'd been trying to solve my whole life. Suddenly, everything made sense. These laws aren't just philosophical ideas, they're practical, powerful forces that influence every aspect of our lives. Once you understand them, you can begin to work with them, harnessing their power to create the life you desire.

There are many universal laws, but in this chapter, I'll focus on the ones that have had the most significant impact on my journey. These laws have shaped my understanding of success, happiness, and personal growth. Each law offers a unique perspective on how the universe operates, and each one has helped me navigate life's challenges with more clarity, purpose, and empowerment.

Law of Attraction: Like Attracts Like

You've probably heard of the Law of Attraction before, it's the headliner in this universal lineup. The simplest way to explain this law is that like attracts like. The energy you project into the world is exactly what you'll get back. Think of it like tuning a radio: if you're broadcasting on the "worry and lack" station, guess what? That's all you're going to hear. But when you tune into abundance, positivity, and success, suddenly everything sounds a lot better.

The Law of Attraction teaches that the energy we put out into the universe, whether through thoughts, words, or actions, will reflect back in the form of our life experiences. It's not just about positive thinking, it's about aligning your entire being with the energy of what you want to create.

Personal Example:

Before I understood the Law of Attraction, I was stuck in a cycle of negative thinking. I focused on all the things going wrong in my life, financial struggles, tough relationships, and feeling stuck. Unsurprisingly, the more I focused on these problems, the more they persisted. It felt like life was working against me no matter how hard I tried.

When I was introduced to the Law of Attraction, everything changed. I started paying more attention to my thoughts and realized that constantly focusing on lack and negativity was only attracting more of the same. So, I made a conscious effort to shift my focus toward gratitude, positivity, and the things I wanted to attract into my life. One of the most powerful tools I used was the "I AM" mantra.

The Power of "I AM" Mantras

One of the biggest shifts in my mindset came from incorporating the "I AM" mantra into my daily routine. I used to watch a YouTube channel called Allisone for meditation, and it was filled with affirmations that began with "I AM." This type of meditation became a cornerstone of my practice. The "I AM" mantra is a powerful affirmation of your current state. When you say "I AM," you're not just speaking words, you're declaring who you are to the universe and what you're attracting into your life.

For example, saying "I AM successful" or "I AM abundant" sends a clear signal to the universe that you are aligning with that energy right now, not at some distant point in the future. The universe doesn't distinguish between what's real and what's imagined, it simply responds to the vibration you're emitting. By repeatedly affirming these statements, you align your thoughts, emotions, and actions with the reality you want to create.

Over time, these affirmations became habits. After learning the Law of Attraction, the "I AM" mantras, combined with saying "thank you" three times, became powerful tools that shaped how I viewed myself and my life. It wasn't just wishful thinking, it was a way to rewire my subconscious mind and align myself with the success I aimed for.

Practical Application of the "I AM" Mantra:

To integrate the "I AM" mantra into your own life, start by identifying the qualities or outcomes you want to attract. Frame them in the present tense, as though they are already happening. Some examples include:

"I AM confident."
"I AM worthy of love and respect."
"I AM attracting abundance."

"I AM in perfect health."
"I AM grateful."

Once you have your affirmations, say them consistently, either during meditation or throughout the day. The key is to believe them as you say them, even if you don't yet see the evidence in your current reality. Feel the emotion behind the words, visualize yourself already living in that state, and act as if it's already on its way.

Gratitude amplifies this practice. I made it a habit to say "thank you" three times after my affirmations. Gratitude raises your vibration and helps attract more of what you desire into your life. The more I practiced this, the more I noticed opportunities, success, and abundance manifesting around me.

Law of Action: You Must Take Action

The Law of Action is often overlooked when people talk about the Laws of the Universe, but it's one of the most important. While thoughts and intentions are powerful, nothing happens without action. The universe responds to movement. Visualization, belief, and positive thinking are essential, but only when they are paired with aligned action will it create real change.

It's like knowing the directions to your destination but never getting in the car. You won't get anywhere unless you take that first step, and keep taking steps, even when the road gets tough. The universe rewards action, not just good intentions.

Personal Example:

When I first started learning about the Law of Attraction, I made the mistake of thinking that all I had to do was visualize what I wanted, and it would magically appear. I would meditate, say my affirmations, and visualize the life I wanted to live, but nothing changed. It wasn't until I realized I had to take action, consistent, purposeful action, when things started to shift.

In my real estate career, I made it a point to take action every single day. I reached out to clients, followed up on leads, and put in the work, even on days when it felt like nothing was happening. The key was staying consistent, trusting that each action was moving me closer to my goals. Slowly but surely, it started. The deals started coming in, relationships started forming, and the opportunities I had visualized began to materialize.

The phone didn't just ring on its own, I had to pick it up and dial. But once I did, the universe met me halfway. Since then, I've received awards and accolades like the Masters Awards and Pacesetter Awards. But none of that would have happened if I hadn't taken the necessary steps to put my intentions into action.

Practical Application:

The Law of Action is simple but often the hardest to execute because it requires discipline and effort. Here are some ways you can start applying this law in your life:

Identify small, consistent actions. Every big goal starts with small steps. Identify one small action you can take today that will move you closer to your goal. It could be making a phone call, sending an email, or researching your next move. The key is to keep moving forward, even if it feels like progress is slow.

Trust the process. You might not see results right away, and that's okay. The universe responds to consistent effort over time. Each action you take is like planting a seed. You have to trust that with patience and persistence, those seeds will grow into the outcomes you desire.

Stay aligned with your intentions. It's not just about doing random tasks, it's about taking action that aligns with your goals and intentions. Ask yourself before each step, "Does this action align with the life I want to create?" If it does, take it. If it doesn't, re-evaluate and find a better path.

Act with faith. Sometimes, you'll be required to take action even when you don't see the full picture. Trust that by moving forward, even in uncertainty, the universe will guide you to the right outcomes.

Taking Action in Your Own Life:

The universe rewards action with momentum. The more aligned actions you take, the more support you'll receive from the universe. Remember, it's not just about visualizing your goals; it's about showing up and doing the work to bring those goals into reality. This is where dreams become real, where the energy you've put into intention turns into tangible results.

Law of Correspondence: As Within, So Without

The Law of Correspondence is a powerful reminder that our external reality is a direct reflection of our internal state. What we experience in the world around us mirrors what's happening inside us, our thoughts, beliefs, and emotions. If you want to see change in your external circumstances, you have to start by working on yourself.

For much of my life, I understood this concept in my career, but not in my personal life. In my professional world, things were going well because I pushed myself. I came to work with 100% effort and didn't expect anyone else to do the heavy lifting. I blamed no one for setbacks or challenges. If things didn't go as planned, I took it as a sign that I needed to improve, work harder, or find a different approach.

However, my personal life was a different story. I blamed others for the difficulties I was facing, circumstances, people, relationships, anything else other than me. It was easier to point fingers than to look inward and ask myself what I could do differently. That is, until I implemented a rule that changed everything: I would only blame myself. But not in a confidence-destroying way. This was about constructive self-criticism, not self-deprecation. It was a way to take ownership of my life and focus on what I could control rather than blaming the world around me.

Constructive Self-Criticism

This new rule wasn't about tearing myself down, it was about learning from every situation. If I could give myself honest, constructive criticism without placing blame on others, what would I say? What could I learn from each experience? How could I grow from it? This approach shifted everything for me. Instead of playing the victim, I became the student of my own life.

In moments when things didn't go well, I stopped asking, "Why did this happen to me?" Instead, I started asking, "What can I learn from this?" This became a powerful tool for growth. For example, if a relationship wasn't working, instead of blaming the other person, I'd ask myself, "What could I have done differently?" If I was frustrated at a situation, I'd reflect on how my reactions and emotions contributed to the outcome. This wasn't about beating myself up, it was about understanding that I had the power to change the dynamics of my life by changing myself.

Practical Application:

If you want to work with the Law of Correspondence effectively, start by practicing constructive self-criticism. Here's how:

Own your responsibility. In every situation, ask yourself what role you played. Even if the situation feels out of your control, there is always something you can learn or a way you can grow. It's not about assigning blame; it's about taking responsibility for your own growth.

Ask constructive questions. When things don't go as planned, ask yourself, "What can I learn from this?" or "How can I approach this differently next time?" By focusing on learning and improvement, you shift your mindset from blame to growth.

Eliminate blame. Make it a rule to stop blaming others for your circumstances. Instead, focus on what you can control, your thoughts, actions, and responses. The moment you stop blaming external factors, you'll see how much power you have to influence your life.

Use setbacks as lessons. Every setback or challenge is an opportunity to learn. Instead of getting stuck in frustration, look at it as a chance to gain insight into yourself and how you can become better. Growth happens when we learn from our experiences, not when we blame others for them.

Focus on progress, not perfection. The goal isn't to be perfect, it's to grow. Be kind to yourself in the process. Constructive self-criticism should build you up, not tear you down. Use it as a tool for improvement, not self-destruction.

Bringing It All Together:

The Law of Correspondence teaches us that our external reality mirrors our internal state. In my career, this meant showing up 100% and owning my actions. In my personal life, it took time to realize the same rule applied: if I wanted change, I had to start by changing myself. By practicing constructive self-criticism, increasing my self-awareness and eliminating blame, I took control of my growth. The more aligned I became internally, the more my external world started to reflect that.

This law empowers you to take responsibility for your life, not in a way that tears you down, but in a way that helps you grow. The moment you stop blaming others and start looking inward, you unlock the power to transform your reality.

Law of Cause and Effect: Every Action Has a Reaction

Imagine standing at the edge of a calm pond. The moment you throw a rock into the water, ripples form, spreading out in every direction. You can't stop the ripples once they start. The only way to prevent those waves is to stop throwing the rock in the first place. In life, it's much the same. Every action we take is like tossing a stone into the pond of our reality, creating waves, causing reactions. If you don't like the waves you're seeing in your life, you have to look at the rock you're throwing.

This is the essence of the Law of Cause and Effect. Every thought, word, or action you put into the world has an impact, a ripple effect that comes back to you. The key to mastering this law is to understand that if you want to change the results, the waves, you must first change the cause, the rock. Whether in your relationships, career, or personal growth, the energy you send out will return to you in some form. You are the creator of your experiences, and by taking responsibility for your actions, you can shape the life you want to live.

I'll share an example with you shortly, that shows this law in full effect, and how greatly my life changed.

Every Action Has a Ripple

The Law of Cause and Effect operates on the simple principle that every action has a reaction. It doesn't matter if it's a thought, an emotion, or a physical action, what you put out into the universe will eventually return to you. This law isn't just about physical actions, but about the energy and intention behind them. It's about recognizing that the choices you make, whether large or small, set off a chain of events.

For example, how you treat others sends a wave of energy that can either build stronger relationships or create tension. How you show up at work, how you approach challenges, even how you talk to yourself, all these things create ripples that come back to you. If you find your life feels chaotic or you're facing the same struggles repeatedly, it's time to examine what kind of "rocks" you're throwing into the pond.

Personal Example: Taking Responsibility

For much of my life, I didn't fully understand the Law of Cause and Effect. I often found myself stuck in cycles of frustration, especially in relationships. When things went wrong, my immediate reaction was to blame others. If a friendship or relationship became strained, I'd distance myself or hold a grudge, convinced that the other person was at fault. It never occurred to me that my actions were contributing to the situation.

But as I started to study this law, I realized something profound: I was often the cause of my own problems. My reactions, emotions, and actions were shaping the very experiences I was trying to avoid. For example, when I felt hurt by someone, I would retaliate or pull back emotionally, which only deepened the conflict. The more I focused on blame, the more tension I created in my relationships. It was a vicious cycle that continued until I made a conscious decision to take responsibility for my own actions.

Once I started applying the Law of Cause and Effect, things changed. Instead of reacting impulsively, I stepped back and asked myself: What part did I play in this? What could I have done differently? This shift in perspective not only improved my relationships but also helped me grow as a person. By taking ownership of my actions and their effects, I began to see more positive outcomes in all areas of my life.

Practical Application: How to Work with the Law of Cause and Effect

If you want to master the Law of Cause and Effect, it all starts with awareness. You have to recognize that everything you do, say, and think creates a ripple effect. Here's how you can begin applying this law in your daily life:

Take personal responsibility. The first step is to stop blaming others for your circumstances. Instead, focus on what you can control, your thoughts, actions, and responses. Ask yourself, "What am I contributing to this situation? What can I do to change the outcome? When you take ownership of your actions, you reclaim your power.

Pause before reacting. One of the biggest challenges is learning to pause before reacting emotionally. When something triggers you, instead of immediately lashing out or retreating, take a moment to reflect. Ask yourself, "How will my reaction affect the situation? This practice can stop negative cycles from continuing and help you create more positive outcomes.

Understand long term effects. Every action you take has long-term effects, even if you don't see them immediately. Whether it's in your career, relationships, or personal growth, remember that what you do today will shape your future. By consistently making choices that align with your desired outcomes, you'll begin to see those results manifest over time.

Practice positive cause and effect. If you want to experience more positivity in your life, start by putting out positive energy. compliment others; Practice acts of kindness; Approach challenges with optimism. The more you put out good energy, the more it will come back to you in ways you may not expect.

Constructive Criticism and Growth

As I started applying the Law of Cause and Effect in my life, I realized the importance of constructive self-criticism. By examining my own actions and reactions, I began to see how I was contributing to the outcomes I didn't want. This wasn't about blaming myself harshly, it was about taking ownership in a way that allowed me to learn and grow.

For example, in moments of conflict with friends or family, instead of focusing on what the other person did wrong, I'd ask myself: What could I have done differently? By focusing on my own actions, I stopped expecting others to change and started changing myself. Over time, this shift helped me break cycles of negativity and build more harmonious relationships.

Bringing It All Together

The Law of Cause and Effect is a powerful reminder that every action we take, no matter how small, creates a ripple in the universe. By becoming more aware of our actions and reactions, we can shape our lives in ways that align with our goals and desires. This law encourages us to take responsibility for our experiences and understand that what we put out into the world comes back to us.

If you want to create positive changes in your life, start by examining the rocks you're throwing into the pond. What kind of ripples are you creating? Are you contributing to the chaos; or are you encouraging peace, growth, and understanding? The moment you take responsibility for your actions, you empower yourself to create the reality you want. After all, the ripples you send out will eventually come back to you.

Law of Compensation: You Get What You Give

The Law of Compensation is closely tied to the Law of Cause and Effect, but it specifically refers to the idea that the universe rewards you in direct proportion to what you give. This law is often described as reaping what you sow, the energy, effort, and intentions you put out into the world will come back to you, only multiplied. Whether it's in the form of financial abundance, personal fulfillment, or love, the universe will compensate you based on the quality of what you give.

The important thing to remember is that the universe is always keeping track. Every kind act, every effort you put into your goals, and every ounce of positive energy you send out is acknowledged. You may not always see the results right away, but the compensation will come when the time is right. The

Law of Compensation is a reminder that nothing you do goes unnoticed by the universe.

This concept is beautifully illustrated in the Bible. Luke 6:38, says:

> *"Give, and it will be given to you. A good measure, pressed down, shaken together and running over, will be poured into your lap. For with the measure you use, it will be measured to you." (Luke 6:38 NIV)*

The more you give, the more you will receive in return. The idea of "pressed down and running over" emphasizes that the rewards often exceed the effort you give. The universe, or, in this context, God, rewards those who give generously, returning their energy in abundance.

However, the Bible also offers a warning about neglecting your gifts or failing to act. Matthew 25:29, it says:

> *"For whoever has will be given more, and they will have an abundance. Whoever does not have, even what they have will be taken from them." (Matthew 25:29 NIV)*

This passage reminds us that inaction, laziness, or misuse of what we've been given can result in loss. If you fail to use your gifts, opportunities, or resources, you may not only miss out on future abundance but also lose what you currently have. The universe compensates those who put in the effort, but also takes away from those who let their potential go to waste. This duality of the law reminds us that you can either grow what you've been given or watch it slip away if you don't take action.

Personal Example: The Turnaround in My Life

I've seen the Law of Compensation in action multiple times. There were moments when I was at rock bottom, facing financial challenges, relationship struggles, and a sense of hopelessness. At one point, I was hounded by collection agencies, my car was repossessed, and I was living in a mobile home, barely making ends meet. I had nothing but debt, and it felt like life was closing in on me.

During this time, I also committed to doing the inner work I started focusing on becoming a better version of myself, practicing gratitude, putting in the work, and giving more to others, even when I had very little to offer. I believed that if I continued to give my best, the universe would eventually reward me.

Fast forward a few years, and the turnaround astonished me. I found myself in an amazing relationship, owning a home; and with my car fully paid off. Not only that, but I had built a condominium complex and saw my real estate career thriving in ways I never could have imagined. I also ventured into the entertainment industry, landing roles in feature films, TV commercials, and even a national TV series. These opportunities weren't just random luck, they were the result of the energy I had been putting out into the world. I truly believed that by putting in the effort and maintaining faith in the universe, I activated the Law of Compensation in my life.

This law showed me that even during the hardest times, the energy we put out will always come back, often in ways that exceed our expectations. The universe compensates those who stay consistent, keep the faith, and give from a place of abundance, even when it feels like they have nothing to give.

Practical Application:

To activate the Law of Compensation in your life, you need to understand that everything you do is an investment in the energy of the universe. Apply this law in your life with a few of these examples:

Give without expecting immediate returns. The most powerful acts are those done with no expectation of immediate reward. Whether it's kindness, effort in your career, or time spent helping others, the universe will return the energy you invest, but often in ways you don't expect.

Focus on the quality of what you give. The law doesn't just respond to the quantity of what you give, but the quality. Are you doing things out of obligation, or are you giving from the heart? The universe knows the difference. When you give with sincerity and genuine intention, the rewards are far greater.

Consistency is key. Compensation doesn't always come immediately, and that's where consistency comes in. Whether in relationships, work, or personal growth, keep showing up, keep giving your best, and trust that the universe is keeping track.

Practice patience and faith. The law works on its own timeline, not yours. Don't get discouraged if you don't see instant results. Trust that the universe will reward your efforts when the time is right. Patience is an important part of receiving compensation from the universe.

Avoid inaction. Remember that failing to act on your potential can lead to loss. If you sit back and wait, expecting life to change without putting in the effort, you might find that the opportunities you once had start slipping away. Take action, even when it's difficult, to cultivate the gifts you've been given.

Give and You Will Receive

One of the most valuable lessons I've learned from the Law of Compensation is that the more you give, the more you open yourself to receiving. For years, even when I was struggling financially, I made it a point to donate to charities, help others in need, and give my time to people who needed support. I didn't expect anything in return; Over time, I started noticing that the more I gave, the more abundance flowed into my life.

Sometimes the compensation came in unexpected forms, like a new friendship, an opportunity I hadn't seen coming, or support from someone when I least expected it. The universe has a way of compensating you when you give from a place of sincerity, without expecting anything in return.

Bringing It All Together:

The Law of Compensation is about understanding that everything you put out into the universe will eventually come back to you, multiplied. If you want abundance, you have to give from a place of abundance. Whether it's your time, your kindness, or your hard work, the universe is always watching and keeping track.

At the same time, you must be aware that neglecting your gifts or failing to take action can lead to loss. If you want to see positive returns in your life, focus on giving the best of yourself in everything you do. Whether in your career, your relationships, or your personal growth, give generously, from the heart. The universe will compensate you for your efforts, often in ways that exceed your expectations. Remember, the more you give, the more you open yourself to receive, and the more you neglect your potential, the more likely it is that you will lose it.

Law of Polarity: Everything Has an Opposite

The Law of Polarity teaches us that everything in the universe has an opposite, light and dark, hot and cold, good and bad. You may have heard me say, "You can't have a top without a bottom, so even bad must have a good." This is the essence of the Law of Polarity. For every challenge or negative experience we face, there is an opposite, a hidden blessing, a lesson, or an opportunity. It's a universal law that reminds us that life is filled with contrasts, and it's through these contrasts that we grow.

Without darkness, we wouldn't fully appreciate the light. Without challenges, we wouldn't recognize success. The Law of Polarity shows us that within every problem is its solution, and within every hardship is an opportunity for growth. Our task is to see both sides of the equation and use this understanding to transform our perspective.

Personal Example: Finding the Good in the Bad

One of the most profound lessons I learned from the Law of Polarity came during a difficult time in my life. There was a period when I was struggling financially, and it seemed like nothing was going right. I felt stuck and overwhelmed by negative circumstances, which made it hard to see any light at the end of the tunnel.

However, as I began studying the Law of Polarity, I realized every challenge contains its opposite, within every problem, there's an opportunity. What does that mean? I started to look for the good in the bad. What was this difficult time trying to teach me? What lessons could I take away from the experience? The answer was growth.

I learned resilience, patience, and resourcefulness. While

the external circumstances were tough, they were shaping me into a stronger, wiser version of myself. This shift in perspective changed everything. I no longer saw challenges as roadblocks but as opportunities to learn, grow, and evolve. Once I embraced the Law of Polarity, I found peace even in the most difficult moments, knowing the hardship would eventually lead to something greater.

Practical Application: Embracing the Contrasts

The Law of Polarity invites us to reframe how we view challenges and setbacks. Here are some practical ways to work with this law:

Look for the hidden blessing. When faced with a difficult situation, ask yourself, "What's the opposite of this experience? What good can come from this?" By shifting your perspective, you can start to see the positive side of any challenge.

Embrace the contrast. Understand that life is full of highs and lows, and both are necessary for growth. The lows help us appreciate the highs, and the challenges make the victories sweeter. Embrace both, the difficult moments are temporary and will eventually give way to something positive.

Use contrast to gain clarity: The contrasts in your life help you attain clarity about what you want. If you experience a situation you don't like, ask yourself, "What is the opposite of this, and how can I move toward that?" Focus on the positive outcome, and the negative experience becomes a steppingstone toward something better.

Trust the process. Sometimes the good in a difficult situation isn't immediately visible. Trust that, with time you will see the blessing hidden within the challenge. The Law of Polarity reminds us that everything is part of a larger plan, and even the toughest experiences contribute to our growth.

Bringing It All Together:

The Law of Polarity is a powerful reminder that every experience has two sides, and it's up to us to decide which side on which we focus. Life will present you with challenges, but within those challenges are hidden opportunities for growth. By embracing the contrasts, you can find clarity and move closer to the life you desire.

No situation is purely negative. If you can find the good in the bad and use every challenge as an opportunity to grow, you'll transform how you approach life. You'll no longer fear setbacks or obstacles because you'll know that within every problem lies its opposite, a solution, a lesson, or a blessing.

The next time you face a difficult situation, remember the Law of Polarity. Ask yourself, "What's the lesson here? What's the opportunity in this challenge?" You'll shift your perspective and find strength even in adversity. Every difficulty brings with it the seed of an equal or greater opportunity. The key is to recognize it and use it to your advantage.

Law of Relativity: Everything Is Relative

The Law of Relativity teaches us that nothing in life has meaning except in comparison to something else. Our experiences, challenges, and successes are all relative to the perspective we hold and what we compare them to. This law reminds us that we can choose how we view any situation by shifting the context in which we place it.

In many ways, the Law of Relativity is about understanding

that things aren't inherently good or bad, they just are. How we perceive them depends on the lens we look through. A problem that seems huge in one moment can feel much smaller when compared to a more serious challenge; Success that once felt distant becomes more attainable when we reflect on how far we've already come.

Personal Example: The Reality of Perception

There was a time when I asked a now-distant friend who spent most of his days playing video games and working low-paying jobs, how hard he thought he was working to find a job. He was unemployed at the time and living in a basement, and he'd handed out two resumes that week. When I asked him how hard he was pushing himself on a scale of 1 to 10, he told me he felt like he was at an 8. I was stunned.

At the time, I was a full-time police officer, raising kids, and trying to start a pest control company. I also thought I was working at an 8 out of 10, but this comparison completely shook my perspective. I couldn't believe that two resumes equated to an 8 in his mind.

Later, I watched a show about a music artist who was pushing himself to the point of barely sleeping for days, as he worked on his career. That was when it hit me, compared to that guy, I probably looked like I was giving a 2 out of 10. It was a wake-up call that made me realize how relative our sense of effort and success really is. What seems like hard work to one person could be nothing compared to someone else's standards.

This is why surrounding yourself with motivated people is so important. Not only are they supportive and goal-oriented, but they also raise your standards. When you're around people who push themselves to achieve more, it inspires you to elevate your own efforts. You start to adopt their mindset, and suddenly, what seemed impossible before feels within reach. Their drive becomes contagious, and you find yourself striving for higher levels of success and fulfillment.

Practical Application: How to Use the Law of Relativity

The Law of Relativity offers a powerful tool for changing the way you experience life's challenges and triumphs. Here are some steps you can take to apply this law in your life:

Change your comparisons. When you feel discouraged or frustrated by your progress, take a step back and change your point of comparison. Instead of comparing yourself to others or an idealized version of success, compare yourself to where you were a year ago, five years ago, or ten years ago. You'll likely see how much you've grown.

Surround yourself with motivated people: the company you keep greatly influences how you view your own efforts. When you surround yourself with motivated, ambitious people, they will support you as well as elevate your standards. You'll naturally push yourself harder when you're around those who are goal-oriented and driven.

Focus on growth not perfection. Remember progress is what matters, not perfection. When you compare yourself to an impossible standard, you set yourself up for disappointment. Instead, focus on the small victories and the ways you're evolving, even if it's at a slower pace than you'd like.

Use contrast for clarity. The Law of Relativity helps you gain clarity about your values and goals. If you experience something you don't like, it's an opportunity to clarify what you do want. Contrast allows you to refine your desires and focus on what truly matters to you.

Reframe challenges. When faced with a difficult situation, compare it to something harder you've already overcome. This reframing can make the current challenge seem more manageable and reminds you of the resilience you've built.

Personal Story: The Hockey Game Insight

I referred to before several years ago after a hockey game, I found myself sitting with a group of lawyers and doctors, reflecting on my future. I had been thinking about leaving policing and setting my sights on something higher, something without a ceiling. When I shared this with them, they were supportive. They said that is great, go for it!

When I had a similar conversation with people living paycheck to paycheck, the responses were different. They called me crazy and irresponsible for even thinking that way. That's when the Law of Relativity really hit home. The perception of what's "possible" depends entirely on who you're talking to and the lens through which they see the world. To some, aiming for more seems out of reach. To others, it's a natural progression.

This experience showed me that your beliefs about what's possible are relative to the people and environment around you. Surrounding yourself with people who encourage growth and possibility allows you to maintain a clear vision, even when others might try to pull you back into their limited perspective.

Bringing It All Together:

The Law of Relativity teaches us that everything is relative to the context we place it in. Your challenges are only as big as the perspective you bring to them, and your progress is only as slow as you perceive it to be. By shifting your comparisons and focusing on how far you've come, rather than how far you have to go, you can find gratitude and empowerment in every situation.

This law is a reminder that you have the power to choose your perspective. You can either focus on what's missing; or you can focus on what's present. You can either compare yourself to someone further along, or reflect on how much you've already accomplished. Perhaps most importantly, surrounding yourself with people who inspire and push you to grow can dramatically shift your standards and help you reach new heights.

The Law of Rhythm states that everything in the universe operates in cycles, there are highs and lows, seasons of growth, and seasons of rest. Nothing stays constant, and everything is in a state of movement. Just as the tides ebb and flow, so too, do our lives move in cycles. The Law of Rhythm reminds us that when we're in a low period, it's only temporary; Soon the rhythm will shift back into a period of growth or success.

This law teaches us to be patient and trust the process. Instead of resisting the lows or feeling like they will last forever, we can learn to flow with the rhythm of life. When we understand that every challenge or low point is part of a larger cycle, it becomes easier to navigate difficult times with grace, knowing that they are temporary and will eventually give way to better days.

Law of Perpetual Transmutation of Energy: You Have the Power to Transform

The Law of Perpetual Transmutation of Energy states that energy is always in motion and constantly changing forms. Everything in the universe is made up of energy, and that energy is never static, it's continuously moving, flowing, and evolving. The key to this law is understanding that higher energy has the power to transform lower energy. In other words, by raising your vibration through positive thoughts, actions, and emotions, you can transmute and transform negative situations into positive ones.

This law is incredibly empowering because it reminds us that we are never stuck. No matter how difficult or challenging our circumstances may be, we have the ability to change them. We can transmute the energy of frustration, fear, or doubt into energy of hope, joy, and determination. This is why it's so important to cultivate higher vibrational states like gratitude, love, and faith, because these states allow us to transform the lower energies that may be holding us back.

Personal Example: Transmuting Negative Energy

There was a time in my life when I felt weighed down by negative circumstances. Whether it was financial struggles, relationship difficulties, or internal doubts, I often found myself in a low-energy state. I felt stuck, as if no matter what I did, I couldn't break free from these challenges. That's when I learned about the Law of Perpetual Transmutation of Energy.

I realized that I had the power to change the energy around me by changing my thoughts and actions. Instead of focusing on what was going wrong, I started to shift my attention to what I wanted to create. I began practicing gratitude daily, even for the small things. I made an effort to surround myself with positive, uplifting people and focused on what was possible, rather than what was lacking. Slowly but surely, I started to notice a shift. The situations that once felt overwhelming began to improve, and I felt more empowered to create the life I wanted.

This law showed me that we are never truly stuck. Even in the most difficult moments, we can transmute the negative energy around us into something better. We have the power to transform our circumstances by raising our vibration and focusing on positive action.

Practical Application:

Recognize low energy states. Start by identifying when you're in a low-energy state, feeling frustrated, anxious, or stuck. These moments are opportunities for you to transform that energy into something better.

Shift your focus. The quickest way to transmute low energy is to focus on gratitude and positivity. Even if your current situation feels negative, find something to be grateful for. Gratitude raises your vibration and begins the process of transmutation.

Take empowered action. Energy transmutation isn't just about thinking positively, it's about aligning your actions with higher energy as well. Take small, positive steps toward your goals. Every action you take in the direction of your dreams raises your energy and transforms your circumstances.

Law of Rhythm: Everything Flows in Cycles

The Law of Rhythm states that everything in the universe operates in cycles, there are highs and lows, seasons of growth and seasons of rest. Nothing stays constant, and everything is in a state of movement. Just as the tides ebb and flow, so too do our lives move in cycles. The Law of Rhythm reminds us that when we're in a low period, it's only temporary, and soon the rhythm will shift back into a period of growth or success.

This law teaches us to be patient and trust the process. Instead of resisting the lows or feeling like they will last forever, we can learn to flow with the rhythm of life. When we understand that every challenge or low point is part of a larger cycle, it becomes easier to navigate difficult times with grace, knowing that they are temporary and will eventually give way to better days.

Personal Example: Flowing With Life's Rhythms

In my own life, I've experienced cycles of highs and lows, times when everything seemed to be falling into place, followed by periods when nothing seemed to go right. Early in my journey, I would get frustrated during the low periods, feeling like I had somehow failed. But as I learned about the Law of Rhythm, I realized that these cycles are natural. The highs wouldn't be as sweet without the lows to compare them to, and the lows always contained valuable lessons that helped me grow.

One particular low period was when I was facing financial difficulties and relationship struggles simultaneously. It felt like a season of endless setbacks. But instead of giving in to despair, I reminded myself that this was just part of the rhythm of life. I focused on the lessons I could learn during that time and trusted that the cycle would shift. Sure enough, after that period of struggle, things began to improve, both financially and personally. I came out of that low period stronger and more grateful for the highs that followed.

Practical Application:

Embrace the lows. When you're going through a difficult time, remember it's part of the natural rhythm of life. Instead of resisting it, embrace it as a temporary season. Look for the lessons you can learn and trust that things will improve.

Ride the Highs: During periods of growth and success, take full advantage of the momentum. This is your time to act, create, and push forward. Use the high-energy periods to make significant progress toward your goals.

Find Balance: The Law of Rhythm reminds us to seek balance. Don't get too discouraged during the lows, and don't become overly attached to the highs. Life is a flow of cycles, and learning to navigate them with grace is key to lasting fulfillment.

Law of Gender: The Balance of Masculine and Feminine Energy

The Law of Gender states that everything in the universe has both masculine and feminine energy. This isn't about physical gender; instead, it's about the balance between the two types of energy that exist in everything. Masculine energy is action-oriented, assertive, and driven, while feminine energy is receptive, nurturing, and creative. Both energies are essential for balance, and we need to cultivate both in our lives to experience harmony.

This law reminds us there's a time to act (masculine energy) and a time to rest and receive (feminine energy). Too much masculine energy can lead to burnout, while too much feminine energy can lead to stagnation. The key is to balance both, knowing when to push forward and when to step back and allow things to flow.

Personal Example: Finding Balance

There was a time in my life when I operated almost entirely in masculine energy. I constantly pushed myself, worked hard, took action, and relentlessly strived for success like I'd consumed three cans of my sugar free red bull. While this drive helped me achieve a lot, it also led to burnout. I hadn't allowed myself time to rest, reflect, or receive. I wasn't tapping into my creative, intuitive side, and as a result, I felt drained. Much like the crash after all the energy drinks.

As I began to learn about the Law of Gender, I realized I needed to bring more balance into my life. I incorporated practices that allowed me to tap into my feminine energy, things like meditation, journaling, and spending time in nature. Not only did this help expand my self awareness, but I also learned that sometimes the most powerful thing you can do is step back and allow things to unfold naturally, rather than constantly trying to force them. This balance between action and receptivity is the crucial component that helps me maintain both productivity and peace.

Practical Application:

Embrace both energies. Understanding both masculine and feminine energies are necessary. When it's time to take action, do so with confidence. When it's time to rest or reflect, give yourself permission to slow down and tap into your creative, intuitive side.

Find your flow. Pay attention to when you feel most balanced. Are you pushing too hard without giving yourself time to recharge? Or are you too passive and not taking enough action? Strive to find a flow that allows both energies to work in harmony.

Nurture your intuition. Masculine energy is logical and analytical, while feminine energy is intuitive and creative. Take time to nurture your intuition through practices like meditation, visualization, or simply being still and listening to your inner voice.

Conclusion: Mastering the Laws of the Universe

The Laws of the Universe are not just abstract ideas, they are the guiding principles that shape every aspect of our lives. Once you understand how they work, you hold the power to create a life filled with abundance, joy, and fulfillment. Each law gives you a unique way of viewing the world, showing you that life doesn't just happen to you, you are actively shaping it through your thoughts, emotions, and actions.

The beauty of these laws is that they don't discriminate; They apply to everyone: they are always in motion. Whether you realize it or not, they are working in your life right now. When you start to consciously work with them instead of unknowingly working against them, that's when everything changes. These laws have the potential to transform your relationships, your career, your personal growth, every part of your life.

My journey with these laws has been anything but a straight line. There have been ups and downs, moments of doubt, and times when I felt lost. But learning to live in alignment with the Laws of the Universe has been the most profound and empowering shift I've ever experienced. I can say without hesitation that everything good in my life came from understanding these principles and applying them.

I want you to know you are never a victim of your circumstances. You are a creator. Life is not something that happens to you, it's something you shape and mold with every thought, every emotion, and every choice. The universe is always responding to your energy, always listening to the signals you send out. The more you align yourself with these universal laws, the more you'll find that life starts to work with you, not against you.

The universe is always conspiring to help you achieve your highest potential. It's up to you to stay aware, make conscious choices, and trust the process. Keep these laws close to your heart, use them as a roadmap, and watch as your life begins to blossom in ways you never imagined.

You are not just along for the ride, you're at the wheel.

Chapter 5

Emotions That Raise and Lower Frequency

AS WE NAVIGATE through life, the universe hands us a toolbox full of emotions. Each emotion has its purpose, some lift us up, helping us to connect with higher frequencies, while others drag us down; if left unchecked. The key to mastering this is to consciously choose which emotional tools we use.

Imagine waking up each day with access to a powerful toolbox, gratitude, love, joy, peace, and forgiveness are all waiting for you to pick them up. Here's the kicker: if you don't choose consciously, the universe might hand you the default tools. Trust me, those default tools aren't always the best, they're like trying to fix a leaky faucet with a spoon. You end up making a mess.

The key to raising your vibration and attracting positive outcomes is simple: pick the tools that lift you up. Emotions are energy, and the energy you carry affects not just you, it affects the people and situations you attract into your life. The higher your frequency, the more you align with abundance, joy, and fulfillment.

In this chapter, we'll explore the emotions that raise your frequency and those that lower it. Understanding how to navigate your emotional landscape is crucial for mastering your vibration and manifesting the life you desire.

Emotions That Raise Frequency

Certain emotions, when nurtured and practiced regularly, elevate your vibration to new heights. These emotions act like powerful magnets, attracting positive experiences, people, and opportunities into your life. Let's break down some of the key emotions that can raise your frequency.

Gratitude: The Gateway to Abundance

Gratitude is the Swiss Army knife in your emotional toolbox. Small but incredibly powerful, it shifts your perspective from what's missing to what's already there. When you practice gratitude, you tune into a frequency of abundance, and that shift changes everything. You start to notice the good things, no matter how small; As you do, the universe responds by giving you more for which to be grateful. Gratitude is like a magnet, it attracts more of the positive things in life.

Personal Example: The Gratitude Rock

When I was teaching policing students, the Law of Attraction quickly became a regular part of our conversations. After I received the book *The Secret* from a friend, Sanela, it sparked something in me, and I couldn't stop sharing what I was learning. One day, my students surprised me with a gratitude rock, a simple, small stone, but it carried a lot of meaning. They said, "This is for you, so you can keep practicing gratitude every day."

At the time, things were tough. Financially, emotionally, it felt like I was carrying a heavy load. But that rock? It became my lifeline. I placed it on my desk, and every time I touched it, I'd say "thank you" for something in my life, no matter how small. Sometimes it was for my health, other times for a good conversation with one of my boys, or just for the fact that I was still standing despite everything. That rock got me through tough times, reminding me to stay grateful even when life felt hard. Every time I held that rock, I felt a shift, a moment where the weight lifted, if only for a few seconds.

Saying "thank you" while holding that gratitude rock became a daily practice. Slowly, things began to change. The gratitude rock might have been small, but the impact it had on my mindset was immeasurable. It helped me stay focused on what was working, instead of getting lost in what wasn't.

Practical Application:

Find your own version of a gratitude rock. It doesn't have to be an actual rock, it could be a small item that reminds you to stay grateful. Put it somewhere you'll see it throughout the day everyday. Each time you touch it or see it, think of something you're thankful for, even if it's something as simple as a hot cup of coffee in the morning. Practicing gratitude helps you shift your energy from scarcity to abundance, and the more you do it, the more naturally it will come.

Gratitude isn't just about saying "thank you;"; it's about living in a state of appreciation. The more you tap into that energy of appreciation, the more life opens up to you. Trust me, you don't need everything to be perfect to start feeling grateful, just start where you are, and let the universe take care of the rest.

Love: Finding Common Ground and the Kingdom Within

One thing that has become clear to me over the years is that love is the bridge that connects us all, regardless of our specific beliefs or how we view the world. I've had conversations with people from all walks of life, some deeply religious, others more spiritual like me, and still others who don't identify with any faith. In those conversations, I've come to realize, despite the differences in our beliefs, we often share the same core values.

I've had some great talks with friends who are devout Catholics, people who are spectacular human beings. They follow the teachings of the Bible, attend church regularly, and live their lives with an unwavering sense of devotion. While I don't necessarily align with all the doctrines of their faith, I've found that we share a lot more than I first realized.

I believe deeply in a Creator, and I also believe that the Creator's kingdom is within us. This is where our paths meet. Many writings in the Bible resonate with me, even if I don't subscribe to the entire framework of religion. I see those writings as powerful guides to living a life rooted in love, purpose, and connection. I believe that you don't have to be religious to be in alignment with that divine source. It's about recognizing that, at our core, we're all connected to something greater.

To me, the Creator's kingdom isn't some distant place we're trying to reach, it's already inside of us. It's in the way we treat others, in the love we share, and in the light we bring to the world. That's where I find common ground with many religious teachings, especially those in the Bible. When I read passages about love, kindness, and compassion, they resonate with my own beliefs about the universe and the energy that flows through us all.

At the end of the day, whether you're guided by the Bible, the universe, or your own sense of spirituality, we're all seeking the same thing: to live in harmony with the Creator, to embody love, and to make the world a better place.

Practical Application: Embracing the Kingdom Within

This idea of the Creator's kingdom being within us can guide how we live each day. Start by seeing yourself as a reflection of that divine energy. When you interact with others, see the Creator in them, too. Whether you call it God, the universe, or something else, know that the source of all good is already inside you, and it's there to guide your thoughts, your actions, and your love for others.

Remember that you don't need to follow a specific path to access this inner kingdom. Whether you find wisdom in religious texts like the Bible or through your own personal journey, the key is to live in alignment with that inner truth. Choose love; Choose kindness; Let your life be a reflection of the divine energy within you.

When you live from this place, you're not just walking your path, you're illuminating it. As you do, you'll inspire others to do the same, regardless of where they are on their journey.

Joy: Finding It in the Unexpected Moments

Joy is funny like that, it often sneaks up on you when you least expect it. Some of the best memories I have aren't from the big, planned events, but from the small, unplanned moments where laughter just took over. Like those road trips we used to take to Florida, packed inside a small car with all of us squeezed in for hours on end. I can still hear the weird screeching sounds from the backseat as we headed to fishing trips, who knows where those sounds even came from? But they always left us in fits of laughter. It's in those chaotic, unexpected moments that joy can shine the brightest.

That's the beauty of joy, it doesn't need the perfect setting to show up. In fact, sometimes it comes in situations that could easily go the other way. For example, imagine you're all dressed up in a nice suit; heading to an important meeting, and right as you step outside, a pigeon drops a little "present" on your shoulder. Now, you could get mad, right? But here's the thing, what if you just chose to laugh instead? What if you saw it as life's little joke, a funny reminder not to take everything too seriously?

Joy is always available, even in the moments that seem inconvenient or frustrating. It's all about how you choose to respond. If you're looking for it, you'll find it.

Personal Example: Joy in the Chaos

I've learned that some of the best moments of joy are born in the middle of chaos or discomfort. Those fishing trips we took were some of my favorite times. Sure, there were moments when everything wasn't going as planned, bad weather, tangled lines, or you ..dumping you off at an island. But looking back, it's those very things that brought us the most laughter. The joy wasn't in things going smoothly; it was in the way we responded to whatever came our way.

Joy isn't about perfection or having everything figured out. It's about finding the humor, the lightness, in the situation you're facing. Whether you're crammed in a small car on a long trip or getting an unexpected gift from a pigeon, joy is there if you choose to let it in.

Practical Application: Finding Joy in the Unexpected

Next time something goes "wrong" or doesn't go as planned, pause for a second and ask yourself, "Is there something funny about this? Is there a way to find joy here?" If you can shift your perspective and see the humor or lightness in the situation, it'll instantly change your mood, and the whole experience.

Don't wait for life to be perfect to enjoy it. Joy is often hiding in the mess, in the unexpected, in the chaos. It's up to you to find it and let it turn your day around.

Why Joy Matters

Joy isn't just about having fun, it's about raising your frequency and aligning with the energy of abundance. When you can find joy, even in the unexpected or inconvenient moments, you send out a signal to the universe that you're open to more good things. That joy acts like a magnet, pulling in more positive experiences, more laughter, and more light into your life.

The next time you find yourself in a moment that's less than ideal, remember, joy is always an option. Whether you're on a fishing trip filled with weird noises, stuck in traffic, or even hit by a pigeon's "gift," always find the reason to laugh, to smile, and to feel grateful. Because joy? It's everywhere. You have to choose to see it.

Peace: The Anchor in Life's Storms

Peace is the foundation, the grounding force that keeps you steady when everything else feels chaotic. But here's the thing about peace: it's not something you wait for when life gets quiet and perfect. Peace is something you create, no matter what's happening around you. It's not about living without problems or challenges; it's about finding your calm center in the middle of them. Peace is the tool in your emotional toolbox that helps you navigate life's ups and downs with grace, clarity, and confidence.

Personal Example: The Art of Resetting

When life gets a little chaotic, I've used a technique I call "resetting." It's my way of stopping everything, finding a quiet place, usually a dark room, and having a nap. That's it. Simple, right? But it works wonders. When things start feeling overwhelming, instead of trying to push through or react out of stress, I just pause. I take myself out of the situation and allow my body and mind to reset.

By the time I wake up, it's like hitting a refresh button. The stress feels lighter, my mind feels clearer, and suddenly, everything that seemed overwhelming an hour ago feels more manageable. It's like I've returned to a state of balance, what the body naturally craves, or homeostasis. It's such a powerful tool and it's available to all of us. You don't have to fight through stress; sometimes, the best way to regain peace is to simply reset.

Practical Application: The Reset Button

You don't have to wait for things to spiral out of control before using the reset button. Whenever you feel life getting a little too loud or you feel yourself over stimulated, take a step back. Find a quiet space, close your eyes, and either meditate or even take a quick nap. You'll be surprised at how effective this simple pause can be. It's not about escaping your problems, it's about giving your mind and body a chance to rest and recalibrate so you can approach the situation with clarity.

Even if napping isn't your thing, just stepping away for a moment of silence and deep breathing can work wonders. Think of it as giving your brain a break from the noise. Peace isn't about avoiding the chaos, it's about learning how to reset yourself in the midst of it.

Peace Is a State of Being, Not a Destination

A lot of us think of peace as a place we arrive at after we've "fixed" everything. But here's the truth: peace isn't a destination, it's a state of being. You don't have to wait until life is perfect to feel at peace. You can create it in the middle of any situation, no matter how stressful or chaotic.

Peace is like an anchor. When the waves of life start to toss you around, peace is what keeps you grounded. It's what allows you to stand firm, not get swept away by the drama, the stress, or the noise. The more you practice it, whether through resetting, taking deep breaths, or finding stillness, the stronger that anchor becomes.

Why Peace Raises Your Frequency

Peace raises your vibration by calming the mental and emotional storms that can easily pull you into negative energy. When you choose peace, you align yourself with clarity, calm, and focus. You're no longer reacting to every little thing that goes wrong, you're responding with a calm, steady hand. And in that state, you're able to attract better solutions, clearer thoughts, and more positive outcomes.

When you carry peace, people notice. Your energy shifts, and suddenly, life doesn't feel as overwhelming. You stop feeling like you have to control everything and instead allow things to unfold with a sense of trust. That's the real magic of peace, it doesn't just make life feel better, it makes you better at life.

Personal Reflection: Peace in the Journey

There's something special about finding peace in the chaos, like sitting in a boat while the storm rages, but you know you're safe because your anchor is strong. That's how I've come to see peace in my life. It's not something I chase anymore, it's something I cultivate from within.

That's what I want you to take from this: peace isn't found outside of you, it's created inside. When you learn to master that, everything changes. You stop being a passenger on the ride of life and start being the driver. You get to decide how you feel, no matter what's happening around you.

The next time life gets loud, remember that peace is always an option. Whether it's through resetting, taking a nap, or simply choosing to step away for a moment, peace is something you can create anytime you need it.

Forgiveness: Forgive the Pigeon That Left You a Gift?

Did you forgive the pigeon that left you a gift? You can. Because forgiveness isn't just about the big things; it's also about the little things. It's about letting go of all the stuff that's weighing you down, whether it's a serious wrong or something as simple as a pigeon using you as target practice. Forgiveness is like releasing a burden you didn't even realize you were carrying.

There's a saying that perfectly captures this: "Holding onto anger is like drinking poison and expecting the other person to die." It's a hard truth, but holding onto resentment doesn't hurt the other person, it only hurts you. It drags down your energy, clouds your mind, and keeps you stuck in the past. The more you cling to anger, the more you poison your own well-being. Forgiveness is about setting yourself free.

Forgiveness is the emotional wrench in your toolbox, it loosens the tight grip of resentment and allows you to move forward. But it's not always about letting someone else off the hook; it's about freeing yourself from the emotional chains that keep you stuck. The truth is, holding onto grudges, whether against a pigeon, a coworker, or even yourself, only keeps you at a lower frequency, making it harder to attract the positive things you want in life.

Personal Example: Learning to Forgive the Small Stuff

I'm not going to lie, when life throws a little annoyance your way, like a pigeon mistaking you for a bullseye, it's easy to get caught up in the frustration. But what good does it do? In those moments, you can either let something so small ruin your day, or you can laugh, shrug it off, and forgive. It's about choosing to free yourself from the things that don't really matter in the grand scheme.

This goes beyond just pigeons and mishaps. I've had to forgive people for much bigger things, things that hurt me deeply and left lasting impacts. But here's what I realized: forgiveness is for me, not them. Holding onto anger or resentment didn't hurt the other person; it hurt me. Same for you. Anger and resentment lowers your vibration, keeps you stuck in the past, and blocks your blessings from flowing in.

Practical Application: Forgiving the Big and Small

You don't have to wait for someone to apologize or acknowledge their wrongdoing to forgive them. Forgiveness isn't about excusing what happened, it's about choosing to release the emotional baggage that's holding you down. Here's how you can practice forgiveness:

Start small. Begin by forgiving the little annoyances in life, like that pigeon or the driver who cut you off. Practice letting go of the small stuff, and it'll become easier to forgive the bigger things.

Release the resentment. Take a moment to acknowledge the hurt, but then ask yourself if holding onto that pain is serving you. Chances are, it's not. Choose to release it and in doing so you free yourself.

Forgive for you: Remember, forgiveness isn't for the other person, it's for you. It's about setting yourself free from the negative energy that's keeping you stuck. Whether the other person deserves forgiveness or not doesn't matter. What matters is your peace.

Personal Reflection: Forgiving Yourself

Forgiveness also includes forgiving yourself. We all mess up. We've all said things we regret or made decisions we wish we could take back. Holding onto self-blame or guilt only keeps you trapped. Forgiving yourself is one of the most powerful acts of self-love and growth you can do.

I've had moments where I beat myself up for mistakes I made. But over time, I realized that forgiveness wasn't just something I needed to offer others, it was something I needed to give myself, too. Forgiving yourself is the key to moving forward. It's not about ignoring your mistakes; it's about learning from them, growing, and giving yourself permission to heal.

Why Forgiveness Raises Your Vibration

When you let go of grudges, you let go of the negative energy that's been holding you down. It makes room for lighter, more positive emotions to flow in. Forgiveness raises your vibration because it frees you from the emotional baggage that keeps you stuck in a lower frequency. When you raise your frequency, you attract better things into your life, better relationships, better opportunities, better experiences.

Wishing someone well, even if they've wronged you. That act releases the emotional ties that have been holding you back. You're cutting the cord of resentment and freeing yourself to move forward with peace and clarity. It's like lifting a weight off your shoulders and stepping into a lighter, freer version of yourself.

Personal Reflection: Wishing Them the Best

I've come to a place where I truly wish the people from my past the best. Even the ones who hurt me. Holding onto anger isn't going to change anything; Yet releasing it? That changes everything. It frees me up to live my life without the heaviness of grudges or resentment.

At the end of the day, we're all just walking our own paths, learning our own lessons. Some people are still carrying their burdens, and that's their journey. But I've chosen to release mine; In doing so, I've found so much more peace. Now, instead of replaying old arguments or holding onto grudges, I simply say, "We're different people. I've learned, I've grown, and I wish you the best."

That's what forgiveness does, it gives you peace, freedom, and the power to move forward. That's something worth striving for.

Jealousy: Focusing on Lack Lowers Your Vibration

Jealousy is like drinking poison and expecting someone else to suffer. It's a destructive force that only harms you, not the person you envy. When you focus on what others have, it pulls you away from appreciating your own path. Jealousy locks you into a mindset of lack, and as the Law of Attraction teaches us, where your attention goes, energy flows. If you're constantly fixated on what you don't have, that's exactly what you'll continue to manifest in your life, more lack.

It's like using a rusty tool from your emotional toolbox. Not only does it fail to help you, but it also makes everything worse by draining your energy and lowering your vibration. Every moment you spend envying someone else is a moment you're not spending cultivating your own blessings.

Personal Example: Reflecting on Jealousy in Real Life

I remember watching an 18-year-old guitar player go on stage for the first time. He was clearly nervous and made a few mistakes, but the audience applauded and supported him wholeheartedly. As I watched, instead of joining in the support, I found myself pointing out his mistakes to the person I was with. I wasn't an expert guitar player myself, and looking back, I realize I wasn't just critiquing him, I was jealous of the applause and encouragement he received.

Even if I had been a great guitar player, that wouldn't have made my response right. The truth is that; we should support others, especially when they're stepping out of their comfort zones. It's the right thing to do. He was out there taking action, being vulnerable, and putting himself in a position to grow. Instead of being envious, I should have clapped along and celebrated his courage. That would have not only raised my own energy but also contributed to the positive energy in the room.

If I want moments like that, moments of applause and support, then I need to do what he did. I need to step out of my comfort zone and go for it, just as he did. Supporting others on their journey doesn't take anything away from your own; in fact, it adds to the abundance to which we all have access.

This experience touches on several universal laws. The Law of Attraction teaches that if we focus on negativity and envy, we attract more of that into our lives. If we focus on celebration, gratitude, and support, we raise our vibration and attract those same positive experiences. The Law of Action also reminds us that if we want something, we have to take the steps to make it happen. Watching someone else live out a dream should inspire us to take action in our own lives, not fuel jealousy.

Practical Application

The next time you feel jealousy creeping in, take a deep breath and step back. Ask yourself, "What am I grateful for right now?" Jealousy is rooted in comparison, so the quickest way to break free is by focusing on abundance. Start by writing down three things that are unique to your journey, things for which you are genuinely thankful.

This simple act of gratitude shifts your attention from lack to abundance, raising your vibration and allowing more positive experiences to enter your life. Remember, jealousy keeps you stuck in a lower frequency, but gratitude opens the door to growth and opportunity. Where your energy flows, your reality follows.

Anger: Holding Onto Anger Keeps You in a Low Vibrational State

Anger is like trying to fix everything with a hammer, it's forceful, blunt, and rarely the right tool for the job. In the heat of the moment, it can feel powerful, like you're taking control, but holding onto anger does the opposite. It keeps you stuck in a low vibrational state, draining your energy and clouding your judgment. While it might give you a temporary release, anger often leaves behind regret and pushes away the peace and fulfillment you truly want.

Sure, anger can ignite change when used wisely, but clinging to it is like trying to hammer a screw, it damages you more than it helps. It traps you in negativity and repels abundance, keeping you from the higher energy of clarity and resolution.

Personal Example: The Weight of Anger

For years, I used anger as my default response. If things didn't go my way, I'd let my temper flare, thinking it made me strong or earned me respect. But the reality? It kept me stuck, weighed down, and isolated. Relationships suffered and opportunities slipped away because I was too focused on reacting with force instead of understanding.

Then I learned something crucial. Instead of reacting in anger, I started to pause. I would step back, reset, or watch how other angry people were being received by those around them. Seeing the discomfort, the avoidance, or the frustration on others' faces made me realize this is likely how I was being viewed when I let my anger take over. It was eye-opening and humbling. That outside perspective helped me shift, because who wants to be seen like that?

When I chose patience over anger, everything changed. I didn't need the hammer anymore. I learned to approach situations with a softer touch, and life became much smoother. Not only did it feel better, but it also allowed solutions to emerge where anger had only created more problems.

Practical Application: Step Back and Reset

The next time you feel anger rising within you, pause and ask yourself, "Is this really serving me?" Chances are, it's not. Take a moment to reset. Step away from the situation, breathe, and reflect. If you can, observe others when they're angry. Watch how people around them react, are they drawn in, or do they withdraw? This is likely how others perceive you when you're in that state of anger.

Practice responding with patience. It's not always easy, especially when anger has been your automatic response, but every time you choose patience, you elevate your vibration. You break free from the trap of low-frequency anger and open the door to better solutions, stronger relationships, and personal growth.

By resetting and choosing a higher path, you free yourself

from the chains of anger and step into a place of peace and progress. Anger may feel powerful in the moment, but true power comes from mastering your emotions and rising above the chaos.

Fear: Blocks positive outcomes by contracting your energy.

Fear is like a faulty tool that short-circuits your progress. It keeps you from taking risks, pursuing dreams, and stepping outside of your comfort zone. Yet fear is also part of growth. You can't avoid it, but you don't have to let it be the default tool the universe hands you. Fear contracts your energy, making it harder for positive outcomes to flow into your life.

Personal Example:

Fear used to run the show in my life. I was afraid of failing, afraid of being judged, afraid of making the wrong move. But the more I let fear drive my decisions, the more stuck I felt. When I finally started to face those fears head-on, reaching into the toolbox for courage instead, things began to change. I realized that fear wasn't my enemy; it was just a signal that I was about to grow. Instead of avoiding it, I leaned into it. I would trust in knowing that every time I pushed through fear, I was raising my frequency.

Practical Application:

Start by recognizing fear for what it is, a natural part of growth. Instead of letting fear paralyze you, acknowledge it and then choose to act anyway. Fear will always be there when you're stepping into something new, but the more you face it, the less power it has over you. Practice courage by taking small steps outside of your comfort zone each day. The more you do, the more you'll realize that fear is just a tool for growth, not a reason to stay stuck.

Resentment: Prevents Growth and Keeps You Stuck in Negative Patterns

Resentment is like holding onto a broken tool, it doesn't fix anything, and over time, it causes even more harm. You might think holding onto it will protect you or make things right, but all it does is keep you tied to the past and stuck in negative patterns. It drains your energy and blocks your ability to grow, trapping you in a low-frequency state.

When you're in the moment, resentment can feel almost impossible to let go of. It clings to you, convincing you that you're justified in holding onto the hurt. I know this feeling well. For years, I resented the person I lived with, and even after that relationship ended, the resentment lingered, affecting me long after it should have. In those moments, it felt like there were no other options, I wish I had known that there were different emotional tools I could have used to free myself sooner.

The truth is, resentment doesn't harm the person you hold it against, it only hurts you. It's like walking around with a heavy burden that weighs you down, keeping you from experiencing the peace and growth you deserve.

Personal Example: The Difficulty of Letting Go

For a long time, the resentment i held toward someone I lived with. It became part of my everyday life, a constant undercurrent that I carried with me even after the relationship ended. I felt justified in my resentment, believing that somehow, holding onto it would protect me from being hurt again. All that it did was keep me emotionally stuck, reliving the same pain over and over.

Looking back, I realize I didn't understand my emotional options. I didn't know there was a way out of that feeling, that I could have chosen forgiveness or at least release. I was stuck in a cycle of negativity, and it kept me from moving forward and focusing on my own growth. Once I learned to let go of that resentment, it was like setting down a heavy weight I had been carrying for years. The relief was immediate, and I finally felt free to focus on what truly mattered, my peace, my future, and my happiness.

Practical Application: Understanding Your Emotional Options

In the heat of the moment, resentment feels like the only option, but it's not. The next time you feel resentment creeping in, pause and ask yourself if holding onto it is truly serving you. Of course the answer is, it's not. Instead of clinging to that hurt, consider other emotional tools, like forgiveness, acceptance, or simply releasing the burden for your own peace of mind.

Take inventory of where you're holding onto resentment. Is it serving you, or is it keeping you stuck in the past? Practice letting go, not for the other person's sake, but for your own. Letting go frees up your energy and allows you to focus on growth and positive outcomes. You may not have control over the past, but you have full control over how you move forward.

Resentment is a heavy chain that keeps you bound to what's already happened. Breaking that chain sets you free to step into a future filled with peace, clarity, and opportunities for growth.

Closing Reflection: Choosing the Right Tools

As I wrap up this chapter, I reflect on the greatest tools in my life, my kids. They have been my constant source of joy, teaching me more about love, patience, and growth than I ever thought possible. I'm thankful for who they are just as they are, and for the support they've shown me over the years. They may not realize it, but they are a huge reason for my happiness. Sure, they're still learning their own lessons, just like I am. But that's life, isn't it? We're all in this together, growing, learning, and figuring it out as we go. For that, I'm eternally grateful.

Final Thoughts on Emotions That Raise and Lower Frequency

Emotions are powerful tools that shape not only the energy you carry into the world but also your physical and mental health. When you choose emotions like gratitude, love, joy, peace, and forgiveness, you raise your vibration and align with the highest frequencies of the universe. These positive emotions are healing, they reduce stress, boost your immune system, and promote overall well-being. In the process, they attract positive outcomes, deepen relationships, and open doors to abundance in every area of your life.

On the flip side, emotions like jealousy, anger, fear, and resentment do more damage than just lower your vibration, they take a serious toll on your physical and mental health. Holding onto these negative emotions can lead to chronic stress, anxiety, and even physical illnesses like high blood pressure or heart disease. Your body responds to the energy you give it. When you stay stuck in these low-frequency states, you're not only blocking the flow of good things into your life but also harming yourself from the inside out.

The key is learning to consciously choose which emotions you allow into your energy field. It's not about ignoring or suppressing negative emotions, but about recognizing when they no longer serve you and releasing them before they take root in your mind and body.

A Healthy Mind, A Healthy Life

We often underestimate the connection between emotions and health. Stress, fueled by negative emotions, weakens your immune system and makes you more susceptible to illness. Anxiety and anger clouds your judgment, making it harder to find solutions. Resentment eats away at your peace, keeping you stuck in a constant loop of past hurts. These emotions don't just weigh on your mind, they weigh on your body too, affecting your overall well-being.

But the beauty is; that just as negative emotions can harm, positive emotions can heal. By filling your life with love, gratitude, and joy, you're not just raising your vibration, you're actively improving your health, both mentally and physically. The simple act of choosing gratitude can lower your stress levels, and embracing forgiveness can free you from emotional pain.

Choosing the Right Tools

The universe gives you a toolbox full of emotions every day, and it's up to you to decide which tools you'll use. Choose the ones that lift you up, the ones that heal and guide you toward a better version of yourself. Remember, every emotion you hold onto is either pushing you toward health and growth or pulling you back into stagnation and suffering.

Choose wisely. Choose the emotions that will transform your life for the better, because when you do, you'll notice that not only your mindset improves, but your body and soul will follow suit. That's the ultimate key to living a fulfilling, vibrant life.

Success: Redefining What It Means

Success is an individual choice; As much as you work and create good habits, I believe success is when you just know your goal is going to happen. The wheels are in motion, and you can feel the plan and work coming together. It's not about a specific outcome or a dollar amount, it's about that inner knowing that what you're doing is aligned with your purpose. Success feels like momentum; like you're moving forward with confidence, even if the finish line isn't in sight yet.

In today's world, there's a lot of competition and pressure to "keep up with the Joneses." Whether it's trying to match someone else's lifestyle, career, or financial achievements, this constant comparison can easily pull you into a negative headspace. Competing with others often leads to feelings of inadequacy and frustration, none of which serve your growth or well-being.

Instead of focusing on competition or external validation, do things for you. Achieve your own happiness, not someone else's version. There's an expression that says, "Do what you love, and the money will follow." I believe that to be true, but it's important to remember that it still requires action. You can have all the passion and love for something in the world, but without action, you're not going to get anywhere.

Success is about aligning with what makes you truly happy and then taking consistent, determined actions toward it. You must not only dream, but also do.

Personal Example: Achieving Your Happiness Through Action

When I first started in real estate, I was laser-focused on hitting financial targets because I thought that would make me happy. But even when I reached those goals, I realized the happiness wasn't there. That's when I started shifting my focus away from external validation and toward creating a life that aligned with what I truly loved, freedom, family, and helping others. Once I made that shift, things began to change. But it wasn't just the mindset shift that mattered, it was the action I took afterward that made the difference.

For example, when my partners and I bought a piece of land, none of us were financially wealthy, and the move immediately put us at a disadvantage. Banks refused to give us loans, but we didn't let that stop us. We kept taking action, moving forward despite the setbacks. Eventually, we overcame the challenges and now own a condominium complex. The experience was tough, but it reinforced the idea that doing what you love combined with consistent action leads to success.

Practical Application: Take Action Toward Your Own Happiness

Do what you love; Success isn't just about external markers like money or status. It's about finding what truly makes you happy and pursuing it with passion. Remember, love alone isn't enough, action is required.

Take consistent steps; No matter how much you love something, if you don't take steps toward making it a reality, you'll stay stuck. Even small steps forward can build momentum toward success.

Trust the process; If you're doing what you love and taking action, trust that the money and success will follow. You don't need to chase it, let it come as a natural result of your efforts.

Chapter 6

The Power of Action

THE TRUTH IS; that you can have all the knowledge, the best plans, and the grandest dreams, but without action, none of it matters. Action is the bridge between your ideas and your reality. It's what turns thoughts into results and dreams into accomplishments. The power of action lies in its ability to transform potential into progress. The difference between those who succeed and those who don't isn't just in what they know, it's in what they do.

Too many people wait for the "perfect moment" to take action. They wait for the stars to align, for every obstacle to clear, or for someone to give them permission to move forward. But here's the thing: perfection never comes. The stars rarely align, and waiting only leads to missed opportunities. The people who achieve their dreams are the ones who act in spite of the obstacles, who take risks, and who understand that failure is part of the process.

Personal Story: Taking Action Even When It's Hard

I remember when my partners and I bought that piece of land, knowing full well it was a financial risk. We weren't wealthy, and the moment we made that decision, we were in the loss column. The banks refused to give us loans, and there were countless reasons to stop. But we didn't. We kept moving forward, taking action even when it felt like the odds were stacked against us. It wasn't easy, and there were moments when it felt like we might not succeed. But the difference between staying stuck and moving forward was our willingness to act despite the challenges.

Eventually, through sheer determination and continuous action, we turned that risk into a reality, a condominium complex that we now own. What made the difference wasn't luck. It was action.

Why Action is Non-Negotiable

Action is non-negotiable if you want to make progress. You don't need to have all the answers before you take that first step. The truth is, you often figure things out while you're moving forward. If you wait until everything is perfectly planned, you'll never start. Action brings clarity, and with each step, the next one becomes clearer.

Taking action also builds momentum. The more you move, the more opportunities appear, and the more confident you become in your ability to achieve your goals. It's like rolling a snowball down a hill. At first, it might seem small, but as you keep pushing, it grows larger and faster until it's unstoppable.

The Cost of Not Taking Action:

While You Play, I Work

I once heard a saying that goes something like this: "While you party, I work. While you sleep, I grind. While you procrastinate, I'm taking steps forward." It's a powerful reminder of the difference that consistent action makes over time.

So many people spend their time in their comfort zones, chasing immediate pleasure, whether that's partying, watching TV, or scrolling through social media. They might even convince themselves that success will come one day, without realizing that success comes only to those who work for it. There's nothing wrong with having fun or enjoying downtime, but the reality is; that if you spend more time playing than working, you can't expect to achieve your highest goals.

Look at any successful person in history, whether it's athletes, entrepreneurs, or artists. They all have one thing in common: they sacrificed short-term pleasures for long-term success. They understood that while others were taking it easy, they needed to be working, grinding, and making progress. It's not glamorous; or easy, but it's what sets people apart.

Famous Quotes on Work and Action

Famous figures have echoed this sentiment. Will Smith once said, "While the other guy's sleeping, I'm working. While the other guy's eating, I'm working." That level of dedication is what propels people toward their dreams. It's not about how many hours you work, it's about the consistency of your actions.

Another famous quote comes from NBA star Kobe Bryant, who said, "I have nothing in common with lazy people who blame others for their lack of success. Great things come from hard work and perseverance. No excuses." Kobe's work ethic wasn't just about showing up, it was about putting in the work when others weren't willing.

Finally, Thomas Edison said, "Opportunity is missed by most people because it is dressed in overalls and looks like work." While some people chase shortcuts or quick wins, real opportunity comes through action and hard work.

Personal Reflection: The Power of Sacrifice and Action

I've seen the benefits of sacrifice in my own life. There were countless times when I could have chosen the easy road, when I could have taken a break or waited for the "right time." But every time I pushed forward, even when it felt difficult, that's when real progress happened. That's when opportunities appear that wouldn't have been there if I had hesitated.

Practical Application: How to Take Action Today

Here are a few ways you can harness the power of action in your life:

Start small but start now. Don't wait for the perfect plan or situation. Take a small step today toward your goal. That small action will create momentum, and before you know it, you'll be on your way.

Break down your goals; Sometimes big goals feel overwhelming, but breaking them into smaller, manageable steps makes them easier to tackle. Take one step at a time, and don't get bogged down by how far away the end result seems.

Get comfortable with imperfection. If you wait for the perfect time or the perfect version of yourself to take action, you'll be waiting forever. Embrace imperfection. The journey is messy, and that's okay. You learn and grow as you go.

Hold yourself accountable. Create a system to keep yourself accountable. Whether it's a friend, a coach, or a daily checklist, find a way to ensure you're taking consistent action toward your goals.

Final Thoughts: Act Now, Adjust Later

The power of action is what separates dreamers from doers. It's what turns intentions into outcomes and goals into accomplishments. If there's something you've been wanting to achieve, don't wait for the perfect moment or the perfect version of yourself. Start now, and adjust as you go.

As Tony Robbins said, "The path to success is to take massive, determined action." That's what will get you where you want to go, not wishful thinking or endless planning, but action.

Chapter 7

Chapter: Self-Worth, Success, and Frequency

The Foundation of Self-Worth

SELF-WORTH IS THE starting point for everything. It's the belief that deep down you deserve success, happiness, and abundance, not because of what you do, but because of who you are. Throughout my life, I've realized how deeply self-worth is intertwined with success. How you perceive your value can dictate the opportunities that come your way. This understanding didn't always come easily to me. Like many people, I had to learn that self-worth isn't about waiting for someone else to tell you you're good enough, it's about knowing it for yourself.

In 1997, I was laid off from my factory job, and that moment became a turning point for me. I swore I would never again be at the mercy of a factory, relying on someone else for my livelihood. Inside, I had this strong feeling I was meant for more, but I didn't yet know how to make that happen. That's when I started using an expression that would become my mantra: "I will succeed, and what you see now is only the tip of the iceberg."

I was determined to be something. I knew I had potential, but up until then, I hadn't fully tapped into it. It was that desire for success, that inner drive that pushed me to start thinking bigger. At the time, I was also in a band called Vertigo Joe. We had just released a single called "Euphoria," and it was released via CD across Canada. It felt like a small victory, a step toward something greater. But then I had to ask myself: Was I really going to be a rockstar? Was this the path I wanted to take?

A Pivotal Moment: Choosing Family and Stability

The answer came to me when I was sitting on the basement floor, my first son in my lap. He was just three years old. At that moment, I knew my life wasn't just about me anymore, it was about him. I needed to provide stability, benefits, and a future that would take care of my family. As much as I loved music, my son had to come first. That's when I decided to pursue a career that would offer that security; Within a few years, I was hired by the Toronto Police Service.

Looking back, this was a crucial point in my journey. I had to make a choice between following the unpredictable path of music or creating a more stable life for my family. This wasn't giving up on my dreams; it was shifting my priorities. I knew I could still pursue success, but it would look different than I initially imagined. That's where self-worth comes in, recognizing that your value doesn't depend on what others see but on what you know to be true about yourself.

Breaking Free from Limiting Beliefs

Most of us grow up being told or being influenced to follow certain paths, go to school, get a job, work hard, and conform to societal expectations. But I've always questioned those norms. Who decided what success looks like? Why should I follow their script?

When I was laid off, it could have been a moment of defeat, but instead, it sparked a fire in me. I knew I had to create my own path, not follow the one laid out for me. For too long, I had allowed others to define what success looks like. Now, I was ready to define it for myself.

The truth is many of us follow a script written by someone else. We're taught to live "by the book," but whose book is it, really? Following the traditional path wasn't going to get me where I wanted to go. To achieve real success, I had to break free from limiting beliefs, the idea that I wasn't capable or that success was reserved for someone else. I began to see that success was actually a reflection of how much I believed in myself.

The Power of Frequency and Energy

As I moved forward, I began to understand the role that frequency and energy played in shaping my reality. I dived into learning about the Law of Attraction and how the energy we put out into the world influences the outcomes we experience. This wasn't just about positive thinking, it was aligning my thoughts, emotions, and actions with what I wanted to create.

Our emotions are like tools in a toolbox. We have the power to choose which ones we use each day. High-frequency emotions like gratitude, love, and joy raise our vibration and attract abundance, while low-frequency emotions like fear, anger, and resentment keep us stuck in a cycle of lack. Once I understood this, I started to shift the way I approached life.

Instead of getting bogged down by setbacks, I saw challenges as opportunities for growth. Instead of reacting to situations with anger or frustration, I learned to respond with patience, positivity, and calmness. This shift in mindset changed everything. I wasn't just reacting to life anymore, I was actively creating it.

Success, Frequency, and the Law of Attraction

I've learned the hard way that success, isn't just about hard work, it's about the energy you put into your work. When I began to apply the principles of the Law of Attraction, things started to change for me. I wasn't just working harder; I was working with purpose and intention, knowing that the universe was responding to the energy I was putting out.

This experience reinforced my belief in the Law of Attraction. Success isn't just about grinding away day after day; it's about aligning your energy with the outcomes you want to create. When you believe in yourself and maintain a high frequency, the universe responds in ways you can't always predict.

Overcoming Challenges and Setbacks

The road wasn't always easy. There were plenty of challenges along the way, financial struggles, personal sacrifices, and moments of doubt. But I've come to understand that challenges are part of the process. They're not roadblocks to success; they're opportunities for growth.

When I lost my factory job, it felt like a setback, but it turned out to be the catalyst that set me on a new path. Challenges are tests from the universe, asking how much you truly believe in yourself. Do you have the self-worth to push through? Do you have the resilience to keep going when things get tough?

The answer to those questions determines your success. Every time I faced an obstacle, I had to make a choice, give up or keep moving forward. Each time I chose to move forward, I grew stronger.

Building a Life Aligned with Self-Worth and Frequency

As I reflect on my journey, I can see how self-worth, success, and frequency are all interconnected. Success isn't something that happens overnight, it's the result of believing in yourself, maintaining a high frequency, and taking consistent action toward your goals.

But this isn't just about my story, it's about yours, too. Self-worth isn't something you have to wait for. It's something you can cultivate right now. It's about recognizing your own value and knowing you have the power to create the life you want.

Success is the natural outcome of aligning your energy with your purpose. When you believe in yourself and maintain a high frequency, the universe will respond. It's not about waiting for the perfect moment, it's about taking action today, trusting the path will unfold as it should.

Chapter 8

Reflection and Legacy

"What will you be remembered for?"

IT'S A QUESTION most people only ask when they're nearing the end of their lives. Why wait until then? Legacy isn't something we build in our final days, it's something we're creating every single moment through the choices we make, the lives we touch, and the actions we take. Reflection is the tool that allows us to shape that legacy with intention, making sure what we leave behind is a life of which we're proud.

Legacy isn't built in the big, grand moments. It's in the everyday decisions, the small acts of kindness, the times we choose to rise after a fall. It's in the quiet moments of reflection where we look back at the road we've walked and the one we still have ahead. When we reflect, we give ourselves the chance to rewrite our story, correct our course, and ensure we are living in alignment with the legacy we want to leave behind.

Reflection has always been an essential tool for me. It's in the moments of quiet; when I pause and look back at my journey; that I truly understand the impact of the choices I've made, the people with whom I've surrounded myself, and the influences that have shaped me. Each factor plays a role in building a legacy, whether we realize it or not.

Some of the most profound influences in my life have come from the books I've read and the mentors I've followed, both in person and through their work. But legacy isn't just about what we take in, it's about what we pass on to the next generation. I want to share my journey, these stories, influences, and lessons that have shaped my path in the hope that they can inspire you, my sons, and anyone else reading this.

The Power of Reflection

Reflection is one of the most important practices you can develop. It allows you to assess your choices, learn from your experiences, and make adjustments. Without reflection, it's easy to move through life on autopilot, never stopping to ask if you're on the right path or if there's something more you could be doing to live fully. Autopilot often leads to someone's life feeling as though they are spiraling out of control, or one day looking back and truly confused as to how they reached some point in their lives that they don't like.

For me, New Year's has never been about resolutions, it's my main reflection day. It's when I take a deep dive into where I've been and where I want to go. This is the day I set my intentions and map out my goals for the year ahead. While many people focus on New Year's as a time for quick resolutions that often fade away, I use it as a powerful day of looking back on my life and making deliberate decisions about my future. Reflection and goal-setting when done with intention have the power to change the trajectory of your life.

Personal Story: Realizing My Worth at the Factory

When I first started working at the factory, I went in every day, did my work, and came home. It was a routine that paid the bills but it wasn't fulfilling. I remember thinking one day, "I have to be worth more than this. This can't be the end of my line." That thought hit me like a ton of bricks. I knew deep down I was capable of more, but I was stuck in a cycle that made me feel like this might be all there was for my life.

That realization became a turning point. I reflected deeply on my life and the path I was on. It made me ask, "Is this really the life I want to look back on when I'm older?" The answer was no. That moment of self-reflection pushed me to start thinking about how I could change my circumstances. I began looking for ways to break out of that routine and started reading books and listening to teachings that would eventually transform my mindset.

I'd heard a comment sometime ago and I often repeated it to myself. ; The comment was about being sixty-five and sitting in a rocking chair and reflecting on opportunities and dreams you followed or let slip away. I didn't want to get to that age and have regrets. I used to think, "At that point, it'll be too late to turn back and revisit missed opportunities." It felt like a deadline looming in the distance. Bruce Springsteen sings about "Glory Days," but I don't want my glory days to be in the past, I want all my days to be full of glory. If I'm sitting in a rocking chair at sixty-five, it'll be because I'm taking a moment to rest, not because my best days are behind me. Heck, I'll still be getting up to play baseball!

Reflection gives us the gift of perspective. It allows us to see where we've been and where we're going. It also reminds us that it's never too late to make a change. Whether you're twenty-one or seventy-one, reflection helps you stay aligned with your values and your vision for the future.

Practical Application: Incorporating Reflection into Your Life

If you want to live a life of purpose and leave behind a meaningful legacy, you need to make reflection a regular habit. Here are a few ways to do that:

Daily Reflections: At the end of each day, ask yourself what went well and what could have gone better. This practice keeps you connected to your actions and helps you make small adjustments along the way.

Yearly Reflections: For me, New Year's is the time to reflect deeply on the past year. I review my goals, assess my progress, and set new intentions for the year ahead. It's more than just a tradition, it's a day of accountability and vision for the future.

Reflection Journal: Keep a journal to write down your reflections. It doesn't have to be formal, just a place where you can capture your thoughts, ideas, and lessons learned. Over time, you'll be able to look back and see the growth you've made.

Chapter 9

Odd Thoughts

HAVE YOU EVER found yourself wondering why the world seems so focused on negativity? Why does it feel like bad news travels faster than good news, and why conversations about fear, lack, or failure dominate so many spaces? These "odd thoughts", the ones that sneak into our minds and take root, often feel like they're part of the human condition. But what if they aren't? What if the way we think as a society is completely backward?

Negativity surrounds us, and it's not just emotional. It has real consequences, on our physical health, our mental well-being, and the trajectory of our lives. We live in a world where complaining is normalized, where focusing on problems is seen as being "realistic," and where success is almost an exception rather than an expectation. Whether we're aware of them or not, these old thoughts have been conditioned into our minds from an early age. Breaking free from them takes more than just awareness, it takes deliberate action.

The Backward Thinking of the World

There's a brilliant concept discussed in Steven Siebold's book, *177 Mental Toughness Secrets of the World Class*, where he compares the thought patterns of the wealthy to those of the average person. One of the key takeaways is that the world often thinks backward. While successful people focus on opportunity, growth, and abundance, the average person is taught to focus on limitations, scarcity, and fear.

This backward thinking is everywhere. It's in the news, where fear and disaster are the top stories. It's in the conversations we have, where people bond over their struggles rather than their successes. It's in the education system, where we're taught to follow the rules, keep our heads down, and not think too big. No wonder so many people are stuck in a cycle of negativity, they've been conditioned to think this way.

The Odd Thought of "By the Book"

Another odd thought I've always questioned is the expression "by the book." What is that, really? Who wrote this so-called book and why are we all expected to follow it? I believe doing things "by the book" has made other people rich, not the ones following it.

The world teaches us to conform, to follow a pre-set path, and to do things according to the way they've always been done. But here's the truth: if you want to achieve something extraordinary, you can't just follow someone else's script. You have to write your own book. When you're constantly trying to fit into someone else's mold, you limit your potential and end up working to make someone else's dreams come true.

Take a look at the most successful people in history. How

many of them followed the book? Very few, if any. They forged their own paths, broke the rules, and created something new. The people who stick to the book are often the ones left behind, while those who dare to think differently rise to the top. If anything, following the book has made someone else rich while the followers are stuck on the sidelines.

I'm not saying there's no value in learning from others' experiences, but at some point you have to break free from the constraints of "the book" and trust your instincts. Success comes when you stop living by someone else's rules and start creating your own.

The Matrix: Why People Stay Trapped

The concept of "The Matrix" is often used as a metaphor for the societal systems and mental traps that keep people from reaching their true potential. It's not just about a fictional world of computer-generated reality; in the real world, the Matrix is comprised of the beliefs, rules, and norms that people blindly follow, without questioning whether they truly serve their happiness or growth.

From a young age, society conditions us to live in a certain way, go to school, get a job, work hard, conform to expectations, and settle into a routine. This "programming" starts early, and it's reinforced by schools, family, media, and the culture around us. We're taught to follow a script written by someone else. But what is this book, and who wrote it? I've never been a fan of the saying "by the book." To me, following that book has made other people rich, not the people following it.

We end up living in this "Matrix" of societal expectations, not realizing there's another way. Most people stay in it because of fear, comfort, and a lack of awareness. The Matrix keeps people locked in a mindset of scarcity, limitation, and compliance, often without them even knowing it.

Why People Stay in "The Matrix"

It's all about conditioning and programming. Society teaches us early on to follow the rules. We learn not to question the script, whether it's how to succeed, how to fit in, or even what success looks like. This conditioning keeps people trapped in systems that may not align with their true selves or potential.

Fear of the unknown. It's much easier to stay in the comfort zone than it is to step into uncertainty. "The Matrix" keeps people in a predictable, routine life. Breaking free means facing uncertainty, failure, and rejection, things most people are conditioned to fear.

Comfort and distractions. Modern life is filled with distractions, social media, entertainment, consumerism, that keep people from realizing they're stuck. It's easy to numb ourselves with distractions, chasing temporary pleasures instead of seeking purpose or personal growth.

Lack of awareness. Many people don't even realize they're trapped. They truly lack awareness. They live life on autopilot, following the path they were told is the "right" way without asking themselves if it's the life they want.

Systematic forces. The forces, governments, corporations, institutions, thrive when people stay in the Matrix. They benefit from keeping people compliant, obedient, and focused on consumption rather than creation.

The Power of Thoughts: A Personal Realization

I used to get caught up in this same thinking. I looked at the world through a lens of limitations, what I didn't have, what wasn't working, and how unfair certain things seemed. It wasn't until I started studying the Law of Attraction and reading books like *The Secret* that I realized how powerful my thoughts were in shaping my reality.

I began to notice a pattern in my own life. Whenever I focused on what was lacking, more lack seemed to show up. But when I shifted my thoughts toward what I wanted to create, even in small ways, things started to shift. It wasn't just about positive thinking, it was about changing my entire mindset from one of scarcity to one of abundance.

Most of us are living in a mental framework of scarcity without even realizing it. We're bombarded by messages of lack and limitation every day, and those odd thoughts seep into our subconscious. But the truth is we have the power to change our thinking, and when we do, our entire world shifts.

Mental and Physical Health: The Impact of Negativity

Negativity doesn't just live in our minds, it impacts our bodies, too. There's growing research that shows how chronic negative thinking is linked to physical illness. Stress, anxiety, and even depression often stem from a constant focus on fear, lack, or failure. Over time, these mental states can manifest as physical symptoms, headaches, high blood pressure, and even heart disease.

When you're constantly thinking in negative patterns, your body responds by releasing stress hormones like cortisol. Over time, this takes a toll on your physical health. On the flip side, when you focus on gratitude, positivity, and growth, your body releases hormones like serotonin and dopamine, those feel-good chemicals that boost your mood and improve your overall well-being.

The connection between mental and physical health is undeniable. Yet, so many people continue to live in a state of negativity, not realizing the impact it's having on their bodies. The odd thoughts we allow into our minds aren't just thoughts, they're shaping our health, our happiness, and our futures.

Breaking Free from the Cycle

So how do we break free from this backward thinking? How do we stop letting odd, negative thoughts dictate our lives and start creating a mindset of abundance and positivity?

It starts with awareness. Become aware of the thoughts you're thinking on a daily basis. Are they thoughts of limitation; or are they thoughts of possibility? Are they focused on what you don't have or are they focused on what you want to create?

Once you're aware of your thoughts, the next step is to actively shift them. This isn't easy, it's like retraining a muscle that's been used to doing things one way for years. But with practice, you can start to shift your mindset toward abundance. One way to do this is by practicing gratitude. When you focus on what you're grateful for, you train your mind to see the good in every situation. Over time, this rewires your brain to focus on positivity rather than negativity.

Another important step is to limit your exposure to negativity. This might mean cutting back on how much news you consume, being mindful of the conversations in which you're engaging, and surrounding yourself with people who uplift and inspire you.

Personal Story: Changing My Mental Diet

There was a time when I was surrounded by negativity, whether it was through the people I interacted with, the media I consumed, or even my own thoughts. I didn't realize it at the time, but this constant bombardment of negative energy was affecting my mindset, my health, and my happiness.

Once I became aware of how these odd thoughts were influencing me, I made a conscious decision to change. I started cutting back on the news, limiting my time around negative people, and focusing on good thoughts.

Chapter 10

Do You Believe in Magic?

HAVE YOU EVER thought about someone you haven't seen in years, and then, almost as if by magic, they suddenly appear? Or maybe you've had that eerie feeling that someone was watching you, only to turn and find their eyes fixed on you. These moments feel like more than coincidence, don't they? They seem to suggest that something deeper is happening in the world around us. Whether you call it intuition, energy, or something more mystical, I think there's more magic in the world than we give it credit for.

We often explain these experiences away as "just one of those things," but I believe there's more to it. Life is full of mysteries, connections, and moments that defy explanation. Maybe we've forgotten how to tap into the magic that exists in all of us and the world around us.

Sensing Energy: The Power of Intuition

One of the most common "magical" experiences is the feeling of someone watching you. You know the feeling, you're sitting in a room, minding your own business, and suddenly you feel the weight of someone's gaze. You turn around, and sure enough, someone's looking at you. How do we sense that without seeing or hearing it?

Science might tell us it's a subtle cue picked up by our peripheral vision or some other unnoticed stimulus, but there's something about this that feels beyond the logical explanation. It's almost as if we're tuned into an invisible energy field, a deeper connection between all of us that we can sense even when we can't see it. The human body and mind are capable of incredible things, and I believe that these small moments of intuition are proof that we are more connected than we think.

Manifesting People: The Power of Thought

Have you ever thought of someone you haven't seen in years, and then suddenly they appear in your life, whether they call, message, or you bump into them somewhere unexpected? It happens more often than we care to admit, and after a while, you start wondering if it's really just coincidence. I remember multiple times actually thinking of someone distant and then poof, there they are. It's such a weird feeling when it happens. I would be more inclined to think it's coincidence if it only happened once, but when it happens repeatedly, you start to wonder if there's something bigger at play.

Maybe our thoughts send out signals to the universe, calling people back into our lives. This ties directly into the Law of Attraction, the idea that the energy we put out is what comes back to us. What if simply thinking about someone aligns our energy with theirs, drawing them into our orbit? It's a comforting thought that we have more control over our reality than we might realize.

The Universe's Energy: Connection to the Cosmos

We often forget that we are part of something far larger than ourselves. We live on a planet floating in space, surrounded by planets, stars, and galaxies that have been careening around the cosnos long before us and will be here long after we're gone. The same forces that govern the movement of the planets also affect us.

Think about the Moon. It controls the tides on Earth and influences the natural rhythms of life. Many people believe it affects human behavior, too, with full moons being linked to heightened emotions or energy. Even if we don't fully understand how, the moon's gravitational pull affects all of us. After all, we are made mostly of water, why wouldn't we be influenced by the same forces that govern the seas?

When we consider how connected we are to the universe, the idea of magic doesn't seem so far-fetched. We're part of a vast cosmic system that we can't see or control, yet it impacts our lives in profound ways. In many ways magic, could just be a deeper understanding of that connection, a recognition of the unseen forces at play.

Synchronicity: The Universe's Magic in Action

Synchronicity is another example of the magic we experience in everyday life. Have you ever thought about something, and then the next day it shows up in a conversation, a song on the radio, or a book someone recommends? These little moments of coincidence often feel like the universe is giving us a nod, as if to say, "Yes, you're on the right path."

Carl Jung coined the term "synchronicity" to describe these meaningful coincidences, events that seem unrelated but carry a deeper meaning when they happen together. These moments feel like the universe is speaking directly to us, offering guidance or confirmation when we need it most.

I've had countless experiences with synchronicity; each time it happens, I'm reminded that life is full of unseen connections. When we're open to the magic of these moments, we start to see them everywhere.

Human Consciousness: Unlocking Hidden Potential

One of the greatest mysteries of life is human consciousness. We've been told we only use a fraction of our brain's capacity, so what if the other 90% holds abilities we can't even imagine? I believe there is far more to our history as humans than we currently understand. Ancient civilizations may have been able to tap into this potential, accessing abilities that we've lost over time.

Perhaps the gods and divine beings from ancient myths weren't so far-fetched after all. We're said to be created in God's likeness, so it stands to reason we might have more power and potential within us than we realize. Maybe the abilities that seem supernatural to us now were once second nature to humans who knew how to access them.

These are the things we dismiss as "magic" today, intuition, manifestation, synchronicity, but what if they're simply part of a higher state of consciousness that we've forgotten how to use? What if magic is just the label we put on the things we can't yet explain?

The Mysteries of the Natural World

Beyond human consciousness, there's magic to be found in the natural world as well. Look at the Nazca Lines in Peru, enormous geoglyphs carved into the desert floor that can only be seen from the sky. No one knows exactly how or why they were created. Were they astronomical calendars? Religious symbols? Messages to the gods?

Then there are the unexplained Marfa Lights in Texas, strange orbs of light that appear in the desert, dancing and floating in the air without any clear source. People have been reporting them for over a century, and yet no one knows what causes them.

Even something as everyday as plant growth holds a certain magic. Plants grow toward the sun, even when hidden in the darkness. They know instinctively how to survive, how to stretch and reach for the light. It's as if nature has its own wisdom, a script that guides all living things.

There are so many things in the natural world we have yet to explain, and we see them happening every day. It's hard not to believe in magic when we observe these phenomena with open eyes.

The Magic of the Stars and Planets

We are deeply connected to the stars and planets, even though we might not feel it. Many cultures throughout history have believed the positions of the planets at the time of our birth influence our personality, our destiny, and even the events of our lives.

Astrology, while often dismissed in the modern world, is based on the idea that celestial bodies affect us in ways we don't fully understand. Whether or not you believe in astrology, it's impossible to deny the awe and wonder we feel when we gaze up at the stars. These massive, powerful bodies are floating above us, part of the same universe we inhabit. The sheer scale of the cosmos is magical in itself.

The stars and planets remind us that we are part of something much bigger, something we can't control. Maybe the forces that govern the movement of the planets have more influence over our lives than we realize.

The Magic Within Us

At the end of the day, the greatest magic might lie within each of us. We have the power to dream, to imagine, and to create something out of nothing. Think about it, every invention, every work of art, every great achievement started as a thought in someone's mind.

We are constantly creating our reality through our beliefs, actions, and intentions. That's the real magic, the ability to shape our world through the choices we make. Every time we set a goal or envision a better future, we are using that magic. When those dreams come to life, it's hard to deny that something magical is happening.

Conclusion: Magic is Everywhere

Do you believe in magic? Maybe it's not the kind of magic we see in movies with wizards casting spells or creatures transforming into something fantastical. But there's a certain magic in the world that can't be explained. Whether it's the energy we sense from others, the people we manifest into our lives, or the strange synchronicities that guide us, magic is all around us.

It's in the stars, the planets, the natural world, and most

importantly, within each of us. All we have to do is open our minds, pay attention, and believe.

Conclusion

Final Thoughts and Words of Encouragement

AS I BRING this to a close, I can't help but feel a deep sense of fulfillment. Writing this has been a journey in itself, a chance to reflect on the lessons that have shaped my life and the ideas that have guided me. But more than anything, this book is a message to you, my sons, and to every reader who finds themselves on a journey of their own.

Life is filled with moments that challenge us, that force us to grow and evolve. What I've come to realize over the years is that those challenges are often the very things that guide us toward the lives we're meant to live. They teach us resilience, humility, and the power of persistence. But most importantly, they teach us that we have a choice in how we respond. We may not always be able to control what happens to us, but we can always control how we react. That is where our true power lies.

If there's one message I want you to take from this book, it's this: You have the power to create the life you want. You are not a bystander in your life, you are the creator. The thoughts you think, the actions you take, and the energy you put into the world all shape the reality you experience. It's easy to forget that sometimes, especially when life gets hard. Even in the darkest moments, the power to shift your perspective is within you.

I've spent much of this book talking about concepts like the Law of Attraction, the power of gratitude, and the importance of raising your vibration. These are more than just ideas, they are tools that you can use every single day to change your life. The key is to use them consistently, make them a part of your daily routine, and trust that the universe is always working with you, not against you.

There will be times when doubt creeps in, when the obstacles feel insurmountable, and when the path ahead seems unclear. In those moments, remember that life isn't about perfection, it's about progress. It's about taking one step forward, no matter how small, and trusting that each step is leading you toward your purpose.

Building Your Legacy

As you move forward in your life, think about the legacy you want to leave behind. Legacy isn't just about what you accomplish or the titles you earn, it's about the impact you have on the people around you. It's about how you make others feel, how you contribute to the world, and how you inspire those who follow in your footsteps.

Your legacy is built through the choices you make every day. It's shaped by the kindness you show, the courage you display, and the love you give. While the world may try to define success for you, remember that true success is living a life that aligns with your values, your passions, and your purpose.

Trust the Process

One of the hardest lessons I've learned is to trust the process. Life rarely unfolds in the way we expect it, and that's okay. Through the twists and turns, highs and lows, and moments of uncertainty, trust that everything is happening for a reason. Even the setbacks and disappointments are part of your journey, guiding you toward the growth you need to experience.

When things don't go according to plan, it's easy to feel discouraged or frustrated. Remember every challenge is an opportunity in disguise. It's a chance to learn, grow, and refine your path. Trust that the universe has a plan for you, even if you can't see it at the moment. Keep moving forward, stay open to new possibilities, and never lose sight of your vision.

The Power of Love and Gratitude

Love and gratitude are two of the most powerful forces in the universe. They have the ability to transform your life in ways you can't imagine. When you choose to approach life with love, you raise your vibration, attract positive energy, and create deeper connections with those around you.

Gratitude, on the other hand, shifts your focus from lack to abundance. It opens your heart to the blessings that are already present in your life, and in doing so, it invites even more good things to flow your way. When you practice gratitude consistently, you'll start to notice that life feels lighter, more joyful, and more aligned with your purpose.

Love and gratitude are not just emotions, they are choices.

Choose to love, even when it's difficult. Choose to be grateful, even when things aren't perfect. When you make those choices, you create a ripple effect that touches every aspect of your life.

A Final Word to My Sons

To my sons, I share this: you are a huge reason for my life's happiness. Watching you grow, learn, and become the men you are today has been the greatest gift I could ever ask for. I'm thankful for who you are, just as you are, and for the support you've shown me over the years. You are still learning your own lessons, just like I am, and that's okay, because that's life.

My hope is that this book gives you insight into the lessons I've learned, the struggles I've faced, and the mindset shifts that have helped me along the way. I hope it serves as a guide, a source of inspiration, and a reminder that you are capable of achieving anything to which you set your mind.

Remember, life is a journey. It's not about getting everything right or avoiding failure, it's about embracing the process, learning from every experience, and trusting you are exactly where you're meant to be. Keep moving forward, keep believing in yourself, and never forget that you have the power to create the life of which you dream.

I leave you with one final thought: The most important thing you can do in life is to take action. Don't wait for the perfect moment or the perfect plan, start now. Trust yourself, believe in your vision, and take the first step. Everything else will fall into place.

With gratitude,
Dad

Acknowledgments

Writing Dear Son has been a journey of reflection, growth, and love, and I want to acknowledge the incredible people who have been a part of my life and have helped shape this book.

First and foremost, to my three sons, your presence in my life has been my greatest source of joy, inspiration, and purpose. This book is for you, but it's also because of you. You have taught me more about myself and the world than I could ever have imagined, and I am forever grateful for the privilege of being your father. Thank you for your patience, your love, and for being who you are. You are my legacy.

To Tajana, the amazing woman by my side, your support, love, and belief in me have been an anchor through every challenge. You have shown me what partnership truly means, and I am thankful everyday for the life we are building together.

To my family, especially my sister, thank you for your continued presence and support. Despite the loss of so many loved ones early in life, our connection remains strong, and I hope this book serves as a reminder that love and energy never fade, they simply transform.

To my mentors and influences, Tony Robbins, Bob Proctor, and the many thinkers who helped me see the world in a new light, thank you. Your wisdom and teachings have been invaluable to my journey, and I hope I've passed on just a fraction of what I've learned from you.

To Ada and Noble Ward, my grandparents who raised me, your influence was profound, and the lessons you instilled in me are at the foundation of this book. Though you are no longer with us, your love and guidance continue to resonate through everything I do.

Lastly, to the reader, thank you for sharing this journey. I hope the words within these pages inspire you to think differently, act with purpose, and live with intention. This book is not just a collection of ideas, but a reflection of the life I've lived and the lessons I've learned along the way.

With gratitude,
Bill McLeod

About the Author

Bill McLeod's journey is a testament to resilience, transformation, and the power of belief. Born into a family touched by loss, Bill's mother passed away when he was just 4 months old. Raised primarily by his maternal grandparents, Ada and Noble Ward, and spending time with his father, William McLeod, and other family members along the way, Bill experienced the harsh realities of life early on. By the time he was young, most of his family had passed, leaving him with only his sister, whom he deeply values and hopes will also find meaning in the lessons he's learned.

Bill's early career began in a factory, but he soon transitioned to law enforcement where he served as a police officer. However, after a difficult divorce that left him with little but his children, he was forced to rebuild his life from the ground up. Despite the challenges, Bill found new opportunities in real estate, a career that has been nothing short of remarkable. He discovered not only a new profession but a passion that has fueled much of his success.

When Bill embraced the teachings of *The Secret,* his life truly transformed. By applying the principles of the Law of Attraction, he unlocked the potential for abundance in his personal and professional life. He met an extraordinary woman, Tajana, with whom he built a life and a future. Together, they launched a development company and even constructed their own condominium complex, among other projects. Bill's entrepreneurial spirit didn't stop there, he also started a property management company and hopes that his children will one day join him in these ventures.

Beyond real estate, Bill found another calling in the world of acting. He landed the lead in a feature film and secured roles in other productions, including a national television series. Acting allowed him to explore his creative side, but his ambitions didn't end there. Bill has also ventured into public speaking, sharing his story and the lessons he's learned along the way, and hopes to pursue more speaking engagements in the future.

Through his life's many twists and turns, Bill has embraced the principles of the Law of Attraction, gratitude, and personal development. His experiences have shaped him into the person he is today, a father, entrepreneur, actor, and speaker, always striving for growth, always learning, and always grateful for the opportunities life has presented.

Bill McLeod's story is one of resilience, love, and the belief that no matter where you start, you have the power to create the life you dream of. His film and television work can be found on IMDb.